Putnam P Bishop

Liberty's Ordeal

Putnam P Bishop

Liberty's Ordeal

ISBN/EAN: 9783337037871

Printed in Europe, USA, Canada, Australia, Japan

Cover: Foto ©Suzi / pixelio.de

More available books at **www.hansebooks.com**

LIBERTY'S ORDEAL.

BY

PUTNAM P. BISHOP.

NEW YORK:
SHELDON & COMPANY,
335 BROADWAY (COR. OF WORTH ST.).
1864.

TO HON. JESSE P. BISHOP.

I HAVE written this poem because of my belief that, in times like these, an American citizen should bring all his faculties to the support of his Government. The rule that, as Poetry is a Fine Art, a poem must be an end unto itself, and be distinguished from an oration in having no outward end, I have ventured to disregard. My aim has been precisely the same that I should have maintained had I been composing an oration. Indeed, each of the two parts was written with a view to its public recitation. This, together with the fact that Part I. was completed before the occurrence of the events related in Part II., must account for the unsymmetrical arrangement of topics. The poem, as a mere work of Art—as an end instead of a means—could be greatly improved in point of symmetry, with little labor. But I have thought it best, upon the whole, to let it stand in its original form.

The pursuit of my object has necessitated the foregoing of several attractive features, by which a great part of our later poetry is distinguished. Among these are the mystic element, which never fails, when ably managed, to awaken a singularly deep, though undefinable, emotion, and the penetrable obscurity by which provision is made for the addition of the pleasure of discovery to that of gratified taste. Throughout, I have aimed at perspicuity. To secure it, I have contented myself with many lines which, to my own ear, have an extremely disagreeable sound. Still, in some instances, I have admitted a shade of meaning different from the one I preferred. I suppose it lies within the capabilities of the English language to express any clearly-defined thought, at once, with perfect precision, and in unexceptionable numbers. But the requisite expenditure of time cannot always be afforded.

You will understand that the fiction of a conclave, in Part I., was introduced for the sole reason that it enabled me to present, more briefly, and more clearly, than I could have done by any other expedient, my view of the motives and designs of the rebel leaders in attempting the destruction of the Union. No further merit is claimed for it. On the contrary, I perceive very plainly that, artistically viewed, it is open to unfavorable criticism.

It is unquestionable that many of our public servants, whom I have not named, have, during the contest, in the exhibition of high qualities, fully equalled many others of whom I have made commendatory mention. Distributive justice, in a work of this kind, would be eminently desirable, if it were possible. Of course, it is out of the question. So far as I have gone, I have endeavored to act justly. I have bestowed neither praise, nor censure, where I did not believe it richly deserved. But enough. This, with all its faults, is the best offering that I can make the Republic at present.

AUBURN, September, 1864.

CONTENTS.

Part First.

I.
Fruits of Unworthiness—Former Joys—Founders of the Republic—Equality—Hopes.................................. 13

II.
The Falsehood—Blindness—A Resolve................... 16

III.
Aggression—Awakening—Rage......................... 19

IV.
A Conclave—Yancey—Toombs—Mallory—Floyd—Davis... 21

V.
The President Elect—Intercessions..................... 28

VI.
Difficulties... 32

VII.
Fort Sumter—Heroism................................ 35

VIII.
The Great Uprising.................................... 39

IX.
Civil War—Magnitude of the Contest................... 42

X.
Bull Run... 44

XI.
Sorrows.. 46

XII.
Victories—Hilton Head—Mill Spring—Fort Henry—Fort Donelson—Pea Ridge—New Madrid—Shiloh—Roanoke—Newbern—New-Orleans........................... 48

XIII.
Army of the Potomac—McClellan—Expectations—Strategy—Peninsular Campaign......................... 53

XIV.
Pope's Defence—South Mountain—Antietam—Buell—Perryville—Rosecrans—Murfreesboro...................... 58

XV.
Unveiling of Characters—Southern Patriots—Foreign Artisans, Merchants, Lordlings, and Toadies—Copperheads... 63

XVI.
Questions—Grounds of Hope—Reasons for Action........ 70

Part Second.

I.
July Fourth—Independence—Danger—Trust............ 75

II.
The President's Announcememt—Field of Gettysburg...... 78

III.
Battles of Gettysburg............................... 83

IV.
Helena—Vicksburg.................................... 93

V.
Port Hudson—Charleston—Morgan's Raid—New York Riots. 97

VI.
England.. 101

VII.
France—Russia...................................... 105

VIII.
Hostile Forces—Love of Money—Cowardice—Impatience—Narrow-Mindedness—Ultra-Conservatism—Party-Spirit—Demagogism...................................... 108

IX.

Foolishness—Wisdom—Divine Favor.................... 113

X.

Statesmen — Counsel — Fruits of Governmental Justice—
The Great Deliverance.............................. 116

XI.

Republicanism... 120

XII.

Vanity—Visions.. 125

LIBERTY'S ORDEAL.

PART FIRST.

LIBERTY'S ORDEAL.

Part First.

I.

Of man's unworthiness the fatal blight
Is felt wherever human hopes are bright.
Its breath assails the gifts which Heaven bestows,
And they are changed to springs of direst woes.
The boons heroic men have died to place
Among the fixed possessions of their race,
Through madd'ning of that bane, are cast away;
Then Night attempts, once more, the throne of Day,
And, if the usurpation is withstood,
The cost is measureless in groans and blood.

With what delight our minds, but lately, fed
Upon the blessings which our land o'erspread!
We saw a heritage of priceless worth
In those great deeds which gave our nation birth.

The aims far-reaching, present ends above,
The wisdom, the self-sacrificing love,
By which our chartered liberties were gained,
We deemed a pledge that they would be maintained.
What joy was ours, reflecting on the power
In which America had grown each hour!
Her rising wealth, her people multiplied,
The westward flowing of her human tide,
The shadows yielding to the reaper's gleam,
And howl of wolf to locomotive's scream!

We saw pervade her governmental plan
The truth of man's equality with man;
And, when we sought what fruits that truth could yield,
A soul-entrancing vision was revealed:
Not hundreds lolling on a lofty seat,
With millions crouching, delving at their feet,
But countless citizens, with heads erect,
The happy throng of Liberty's elect,
Ascending, side by side, the sacred height
Which glows all gorgeously in wisdom's light.

And then we saw, with hearts still more elate,
The Church of Christ unfettered by the State.
With course all free, the truths divinely taught,
By their intrinsic force, were claiming thought,
And in the lives of men, from hour to hour,
Disclosing more and more their saving power.
Not now a thing of fashion, form, or law,
Religion to herself restored we saw.

O, we believed that, in our native land,
These springs of blessedness would still expand,
Till every Christian people of the earth
Would fitly estimate their matchless worth,
And, by America's attractive force,
Be moved to follow in the upward course.

II.

But Sin was pressing, all the while, a lie,
Albeit there was a God of truth on high.
Before the minds of men had clearly seen
Of Christian rectitude the light serene,
America, as all the world, received,
And in a dull, unsearching way, believed
The most atrocious falsehood ever told,—
That God's own children may be bought with gold;
And when in full effulgence shone the light,
Disclosing all the majesty of Right,
The eyes of selfishness with piercing pain
Were quickly closed, and all was dark again.

Thus spake the darkened hearts: "What! give up all
This wealth in flesh and blood, which ours we call,
And toil ourselves upon our spreading lands,
Or pay our gold for toil of other hands?
No more to look upon the sable throng,
And feel that all, yes, all to us belong?
It cannot be; and now we say to God,
A single stroke of His avenging rod,
For bondage of His sons, on none must light;
For we intend to prove that bondage right."

They thought the Holy One had given heed,
And rightfulness of hellish wrong decreed;
For, with long-suffering their hearts to draw,
He still delayed to execute His law.
With swelling pride they saw the fertile soil
Respond profusely to the stolen toil.
The fruits of sweat, and blood, and pains untold
Gave place to ever-growing heaps of gold.
They saw their blooming fields stretch far and wide,
And their immortal beings multiplied;
And, in this wickedly attained estate,
Each look and tone said, " We are very great."

How stalk the chiefs of this enslaving class,
Their hearts of flinty rock, their brows of brass!
What measureless contempt on all they throw
Who have no cow'ring human herds to show!
Who ranks with such, however pale his face,
Is of an infinitely lower race.

What do these men on this Republic's soil,
Which proffers manhood's rights to honest toil?
The name " Republic," they salute with sneers,
And then they whisper in each other's ears:
" How pitiful the folly of that fool,
Who does not know that we are born to rule!
They all will know it by and by, but whist!
These thoughts divulged too soon, our mark is missed.
With cunning secrecy our way we'll feel,
Avowing loud our democratic zeal,

And swearing solemnly, in Heaven's high name,
To make the great Republic's weal our aim,
Till we shall gain the strength to overthrow
This cursed Government, that lifts the low,
And in our own supremacy shall stand,
The known, acknowledged masters of this land,
With Slavery's banner waving high in air,
Respected, feared, and lauded everywhere."

III.

Too well those arts have thrived, for guilt so black
In thickest darkness could conceal its track;
And when impunity had made it bold,
And more, and ever more, its aims were told,—
When threats were made to work the nation's death,
They counted still as boastful, empty breath.
'Twas not believed, in passion's wildest storm,
That devils walked the earth in human form.
For peace good men were willing to concede;
For power bad men to each demand agreed;
And thus the blood-stained oligarchy grew,
And pressed, from day to day, exactions new.

At length America's true sons awoke;
The frightful truth upon their vision broke;
They saw with steady sweep the cloud approach,
And Slavery's gloom on Freedom's light encroach;
They heard their fathers calling from above,
Conjuring them, by all that patriots love,
With peaceful ballots armed, to take their stand,
And save from tyranny their native land.

They heard, and they obeyed, and then the rage!
No beasts of prey escaping from their cage,
With hunger furious, or mad with pain,
E'er screamed, and howled, and whirled, and dashed amain,
Like Slavery's lords when freemen were so bold,
And dared to say, with quiet firmness, "Hold!"

IV.

A METHOD in their madness soon was seen.
For anger's thorough frankness quite too mean,
The traitor-chiefs, with swift, but stealthy tread,
And crouching forms, to midnight conclave sped.
Let fancy now, as hearers, place us there,
Of words ofttimes repeated otherwhere.

When all the doors were barred, and 'twas assured
That none could hear save men by treason lured,
While from his eyes the gleams of cunning broke,
With low, yet eager utt'rance Yancey spoke:
"The hour has come, the hour so long desired;
The Southern heart must now be quickly fired;
From State to State our orators must rush,
And let the flames of madd'ning passion gush
O'er all the throngs that, startled by the shock,
To learn its cause will frantically flock.

"We'll tell them all their rights will soon be gone;
That now destruction's gulf begins to yawn;
For, in their victory, the Yankees boast
'Tis their intent to send a mighty host
Of old John Browns, to set the negroes free,

While maids and matrons are compelled to flee
Through forest dark, to reptile-haunted cave,
Themselves from death, or worse than death, to save.
Thanks to our freedom from those cursèd schools,
So crippling to the managers of fools,
We easily shall full belief obtain,
And thus the end of our aspirings gain."

Sly winks and leers commended Yancey's close,
And then the swarthy bully, Toombs, arose.
With rocking form he wore a drunken scowl;
His voice now seemed a grunt, and now a howl.
"That's right," he said; "we'll all go in for that;
If anybody won't, I'll knock him flat.
And now, Sirs, I will tell you something more:
I'll go to-morrow, on the Senate's floor,
And tell the Yankees, if they wish to find
A first-class rebel, body, heart, and mind,
I am the man they seek. O, how I hate
The scamps that try to be so learned, and great,—
The men we've had to fawn upon,—the fools
We've been obliged to wheedle into tools!

"I hate the whole concern. I want to smash
The Government, and hear the falling crash
Of every pillar that supports a frame,
Which even is republican in name.
To think that all must vote, and read, and write,
And hold their heads so proudly in our sight,
And talk so pompously of being free,

As if they thought themselves as good as we!
We've had to bear it, but we'll show them now
Their rascal necks were only made to bow."

As reeled the bully, foaming, to his seat,
The fox-eyed Mallory was on his feet:
"The heart," said he, " of every Southern chief
Must have a foretaste now of sweet relief
In knowing that the hour is near at hand,
When Slavery's noble champions shall stand
In their exclusive dignity and might,
And other men shall cease to claim the right,
As equals, on their footing to appear,
Or in affairs of state to interfere.

"But I submit, if it were wisdom's choice
At once to give our thoughts and wishes voice.
If Southern men our aims too soon shall know,
That knowledge will become our direst foe.
We must be fitted for a deadly strife,
Before we can attempt the nation's life;
We must have time our energies to wake,
And posture for the serpent-spring to take;
And still the Government, with greatest care,
Must be disabled fitly to prepare.

"'Tis plain, the only way of safety lies
In wearing still republican disguise,
And still remaining at our posts of trust,
The requisite machinery to adjust.

The Government will then our wages pay
While her foundation stones we dig away,
And all the people of the North will think
Secession from the earth about to slink;
For stupid Puritans will ne'er suspect
That, under oath to keep, obey, protect
The Constitution in its pristine power,
We're swiftly drawing on its final hour."

Then Secretary Floyd, with sparkling eyes,
Which told how fully he could sympathize
With meanness, forward sprang, and thus he spoke:
"The language of my honored friend awoke
Some thoughts and some conceptions in my mind,
Which possibly you may of value find.
Since I control the military force,
And weak Buchanan gives my will free course,
What soldiers I'm not able to seduce,
I easily can make of little use
By scatt'ring them, at distant points, in squads,
To fall before our overwhelming odds.
The arms and all munitions I will steal,
And in the arsenals of the South conceal.

"I'll take it, too, upon myself to see
That Toucey's conduct shall with mine agree;
The ships of war shall all be sent away,
For sailors can't be trusted to betray.
O, yes; I'll be a servant good and true,
And teach the world there is a service new:

While paid and sworn for Union's health to care,
Her vitals from their fastenings I'll tear."

Loud cheers were heard, and still some faces wore
A look which told that this was something more
Than had been counted on, and that it cost
A struggle to regard as virtues lost
The honesty, and loyalty, and truth,
Which seemed so beautiful to joyous youth.

But soon each voice was hushed, and fixed each eye;
For now, with air imperious and high,
The form emaciate of DAVIS rose.
His thin, white lips were set in firmest close,
And rays, as of a soul-consuming fire,
Were kindling in his eyes a menace dire.
With voice sepulchral, yet made strong by will,
He speaks to men as frozen corpses still.

His words are these: "So far as they extend,
The views expressed befit our lofty end;
But we may well desire to know at first
What is before us, and expect the worst.
Too low an estimate, by far, you make
Of what 'twill cost the Union's bond to break,
And make the people of the South content
To see the fondly loved connection rent,—
To set the prayers of Washington at naught,
And spurn the flag for which their fathers fought.

"Deception can do much, 'tis very true;
And we must daily have a falsehood new
To serve as fuel for their passions' flame,
And keep concealed our own exalted aim.
But this will not suffice; for some there are
Of all the truths which we deny aware,
And firm in their resolves to counterwork
The purposes which in our bosoms lurk.
For these there must be force. No weakness now;
Beneath our rule their stubborn necks must bow;
Or, if they still will carry them so high,
Throughout the South a tree is always nigh.
Yes, Gentlemen, through all the South's domain,
At once we must establish Terror's reign;
The dungeon and the hangman's cord shall teach
No gospel can be held save that we preach.

" 'Twere utter senselessness if we should hope,
Unaided, with the Government to cope,
And win success. But yet we shall succeed;
For be assured that French and English greed
In our behalf will quickly interpose,
And make us masters of our Northern foes.
Those nations now their independence sing,
But they will learn that Cotton is their King.
Besides, all haters of the populace
At once our cause will eagerly embrace.
The Great Republic is the horrid thing
Whose fall their acme of delight would bring.

"And other allies yet we shall secure,
Whose aid will make our triumph swift and sure:
I mean that Northern toadies, fools, and knaves,
As heretofore, will be our fawning slaves.
Then let us quickly to our work, my friends,
With all the zeal which high ambition lends;
Throw superstitious scruples to the wind,
And do and dare whate'er we needful find."

There was a plausive murmur, but no word
Of farther counsel; Davis had been heard,
And 'twas enough. The traitors, one by one,
Began to move, their cloaks and hats put on,
And singly, or in couples, sneaked away,
To set their hellish enginery in play.
As Davis went, he muttered to his heart:
"These senseless villains all expect a part
In that dominion which shall proudly rise
On ruins of the Union they despise.
Well, let them feed upon the hope awhile,
And thus their hours of toil for me beguile;
But soon to all the world it shall be known,
That all the power is mine, and mine alone."

V.

Be traitorous ambition shut from view,
And trace affections of another hue.
For westward from Atlantic's waves, where spread
The treeless plains which lately felt the tread
Of bison herds, as, thundering along,
They sought a shelter from the red-skinned throng,
The men and women of a town are seen
Around a man of unpretending mien,
Who stands in attitude to bid adieu
To friends, long known, and tried, and proven true.

This man is of the people; from his youth,
Attentive ever to the voice of truth,
And ever prompt in act, his soul has wrought
With forces from his country's genius caught.
And now he has the people's high command,
To take his post as chieftain of the land,
And save from fearfulest of overthrows
The Government, to which himself he owes.
His head is bowed; a mighty nation's fate
Oppresses him with all its mountain weight.
And yet of faltering there is no sign:
His brow expresses strength in every line.

His steady gaze bespeaks a soul aware
Of peril dire, yet braced its load to bear.

He speaks, in words which pure affection lends,
Of separation from his trusted friends,
And then, in tones of solemn depth, declares
No human power sufficient for the cares
Which soon on him shall roll. But now he stops;
He wrestles with his heart; at last he drops
The rein, and lets the strong emotion gush,
And all its tokens to his visage rush,
While earnestness each tearful eye distends,
And he exclaims, "O, pray for me, my friends!"
"We will! we will!" with one accord they cry;
"O God! send down thy Spirit from on high,
To strengthen with Thy might, and richly bless,
Thy servant in his work of righteousness."

Nor then, nor from those heaving breasts alone,
Ascends that imploration to the Throne:
A thousand ways the lightning couriers bear
The noble words of Lincoln through the air;
Now click the types, now stand in solid forms;
The wheezing engines move their pond'rous arms,
And wildly hurl about the smoking sheets;
And now the boys are shouting through the streets;
And now a million eager eyes are bent,
To search the President's supreme intent.
O, how the hearts of Christian patriots burn
With sudden, rich delight as they discern

That he would stand with Jesus in accord,
And stay himself upon Creation's Lord.
Their hands are clasped; spontaneously raise
Their thankful hearts the sacrifice of praise.

When evening wanes, the father takes the Book,
With deep, and strange emotion in his look,
And reads, in tones beyond the reach of art,
The promises divine which fill his heart.
Around the altar of the home they kneel,
And blended souls present a joint appeal.
Most fervently they pray that he, who goes
To stand between the Union and her foes,
May soon prevail, by heavenly power upheld,
By love to God, and love to man impelled.
The supplication ended, as they rise,
The light of confidence illumes all eyes;
And, when they singly ask for nightly care,
Each child for "Mr. Lincoln" lisps a prayer.

When comes the sacred day, and Christian throngs
Unite before the Lord their thankful songs,
The souls of Christ's ambassadors, in prayer,
Go near the awful Throne, and wrestle there,
That marks of wrath divine may not descend;
That God a pitying regard may bend;
That He may still a sinful nation spare;
That He may still vouchsafe paternal care;
That He may now enlighten and uphold,
And in the ways of righteousness make bold.

The country's chief, who knows so well his need
Of all the heavenly aid for which they plead.
As from ten thousand pulpits to the skies,
In earnest accents, these petitions rise,
A million agonizing spirits cry:
"Do not, O God! do not the boon deny!"

VI.

Ah! true indeed was that which Lincoln said:
"I cannot hope success without His aid,
Who guided and who strengthened Washington;
Reliance must be fixed on Him alone."
For see! on every side is Treason's work;
In every secret nook her agents lurk;
Her poisonous breath has blasted faith and truth
In matron, maiden, veteran, and youth.
Secessionists are poor who boast but lies;
They must be perjured if they hope to rise.
Such perjured men the chiefs of State surround,
And in the places of high trust are found.
Each plan devised to thwart the traitors' aims,
With all particulars of dates, and names,
Is speedily to traitor-chiefs revealed,
By spies beneath official oaths concealed.

The cunning schemes the Government to rob,
Through treachery of Toucey, Floyd, and Cobb,
And their base underlings, so well have thrived,
That now they see the Government deprived
Of power to raise a minatory hand,
Or e'en herself with steadiness to stand.

By hundreds, men whom she has reared, and taught
How battles for her honor should be fought,
Are stealing through the darkness of the night,
For her disgrace a shameful faith to plight.

But surely cheering to the President
Are words across the heaving ocean sent.
The cultivated, philanthropic men,
For liberty so free with tongue and pen,
From whom such withering rebukes have come,
Because America is Slavery's home,
They certainly will lift their voices high,
And with a matchless earnestness will cry:
"Awake! O, ye Americans, awake!
Your spirits from their baneful stupor shake;
To rescue of your country's freedom rush;
The power of mad, rebellious Slavery crush!"

Since man first looked inquiringly at man,
No expectation ever was more vain.
There live a Gasparin, a Mill, a Bright,
A few beside, who know and love the right.
But who can hear these single voices, drowned
In that o'erwhelming flood of vocal sound,
That choral cry: "Go on, O traitors, on!
Success is yours; the Great Republic's gone!"

Nor ended here the pressure toward despair
On those who held the governmental care.
As servants, not as potentates, they wrought,

And at their hands the common good was sought,
While they controlled no forces for that end,
Save those the people might elect to lend.
How sounded then the country's sovereign voice?
In that dark hour, what was the people's choice?
They had no choice. The minds unused to scan
Aught worse than common wickedness of man,
Were impotent their plans to penetrate
Who viewed their country with a bitter hate.
The people gave the Government no proof
Of readiness to serve their own behoof.

VII.

In very deed, a God was needed then;
The time had fully come to "cease from men;"
And soon in glowing light it was revealed,
That, while from every human eye concealed,
The Providence, so oft besought in prayer,
Had answered with a patient, watchful care.

In that proud city of the Southern coast
Wh'ere Slavery's glories have been vaunted most,—
Where Slavery's venom has performed its worst,
In making patriotic zeal accursed,—
Where Slavery's foul conspiracy began,
The Sovereign has prepared Himself a man:
To Anderson Kentucky's noble son,
Is clearly shown the work which must be done.
Of faithful ones he has a little band,
And each till death will by that banner stand,
Which now, with heaving breasts and sparkling eyes,
They see above the walls of Sumter rise.

There's rage in Charleston when the mid-day sun
Writes on the stripes: "A noble deed is done."
The signs of loyalty, which there appear,

Show Treason's infamy in light too clear;
And that which speaks of honor's worth they swear
Shall wave no more in Carolina's air.
In stately form the Governor demands
That Sumter's keys be given to his hands,
And fair America acknowledge lost
The massive walls erected at her cost.

But fair America falls not so low,
For Anderson asks God, and God says, "No."
The voice divine he tranquilly obeys,
Though treason's camp-fires now around him blaze,
And wheresoe'er he turns his anxious eyes,
He sees the batteries of treason rise,
And Moultrie, crazed by arts of Belial's sons,
Her sister menaces with big-mouthed guns.

And now the little band of heroes see
A foe more frightful than grim cannonry:
The skinny hand of Famine meets each eye;
She screeches out, "Ye madmen, fly!
Bewitched no longer by your country's charms,
But find your safety in rebellion's arms."
Unmoved by this appeal, the faithful band
Await the pointing of the heavenly hand.
They wait not long; past are the numbered days,
And now the wrath of man the Lord shall praise.

As, in the April morning's early light,
The watchman on the walls directs his sight

Across the tide that laves the western shore,
The earth is seen a snowy cloud to pour
Upon the air, and, with a thunder-crash,
Secession's bolts at Union's emblem dash.
The die is cast; and now, with hellish rage,
Blood-thirsty traitors in the work engage;
From Moultrie's face, from South, from West, from North,
The brazen throats their fury bellow forth;
The pond'rous missiles rock the solid walls,
And bursting shell to shell descending calls.

Ten thousand men one hundred men assail;
O, what can efforts of so few avail?
Does not the starry flag at once descend,
And Union to Secession's pleasure bend?
The starry flag still waves its ample folds,
And Union still her upright posture holds;
Her enemies mistook her peaceful mien,
And now her martial aspect shall be seen.

Ye souls of patriots, behold this band!
The hands are few, but each a hero's hand;
And now, from casemate and from parapet,
The fierce assaults are with defiance met.
To Sumter's brow there springs a wreath of smoke;
Around her shoulders is a fiery cloak;
Her frame with mighty indignation shakes,
And at her voice the lurid water quakes.
The spirit of America informs

Her every part, and with this fury storms;
The Nation thunders now to traitor-hearts:
"I will not perish by satanic arts."

From morn to eve, from eve to morn again,
Before ten thousand stand those hundred men;
And, far upon his second course, the sun
Beholds high deeds for Union's honor done.
The flames are bursting from the fortress' crown,
And coals of fire are thickly showering down.
The pallid men are seen to gasp and choke,
In heated air and suffocating smoke.
Yet no one rests; no one a moment stops;
No tongue a word of heart-exhaustion drops.
As nearer comes the raging of the flames,
The guns are pointed with still surer aims;
'Tis but a little while those guns can speak,
But while they can, their voice shall not be weak.

Ah! well that day's decisive work was done;
Eternal honor to thee, Anderson!
Be ever honored, ye heroic men,
Who bought such honor for your country then.

VIII.

As northward flashes, o'er the slender wires,
The glare of traitor and of patriot fires,
A nation wakes, as by an earthquake shock,
To feel the basis of its being rock.
Now twenty million hearts alike are stirred;
From twenty million mouths one cry is heard:
"What! fire upon the old star-spangled flag,
And in its place hang out their filthy rag?
Attempt the Government to overthrow,
And lay our matchless Constitution low?
The nation into jarring fragments break?
Of all our hopes this shameful issue make?
Shall we behold, from her proud station hurled,
America the hissing of the world,
And for the lovers of mankind prepare,
By our base fall, the chalice of despair?
It shall not be. Ye men of seventy-six,
Your gaze serene upon your children fix,
And hear them vow the Government you gave,
From foes without, and foes within, to save."

Now Lincoln sees the people have a choice,
And wait impatiently to hear his voice.

The call to arms no longer is delayed,
Nor sooner sounded forth than 'tis obeyed.
From counting-house, mechanic's shop, and farm,
From pulpit, bench, and lawyer's desk they swarm,
And make each city and each village street
Resound with loud hurrahs, and tramping feet.
The drum and fife send forth their stirring notes;
O'er every house the Union's banner floats;
On every form are seen Red, White, and Blue,
And none finds beauty in another hue.

Gray-bearded men and smooth-chinned boys are seen
Against the walls, with choking sobs, to lean,
O'erwhelmed because the officers reply:
"You cannot for your native country die."

A wife is hanging on her husband's neck,
And struggling mightily her grief to check.
She conquers now; she looks into his eyes,
Prepared far more than life to sacrifice;
She speaks: "My husband, yes; I will consent,
Though God alone sees how this heart is rent.
When you and I are sleeping with the dead,
These precious boys must never hear it said:
'A peril dire your country overhung,
But still your father to his fireside clung.'"

The widow from her closet comes, to meet
The only son, whose gazes still entreat:
Her voice is calm; she gently says: "My son,

Through grace divine, I have the victory won,
And in my feelings there is wrought a change.
A mother's heart is something very strange:
I never loved you so, nor was so proud,
As since I last before my Father bowed.
I've whispered to my soul, with sweetest joy,
'I have a brave and patriotic boy;'
And God forbid a mother's selfishness
A son's nobility should e'er repress."

IX.

Are these things so?   Are these things as they seem?
Are we in civil war?   Do we not dream?
O, real as the grave, as sin, as woe,
As horridest of facts that man may know,
Are all these sights and sounds.   The fire whose glare,
In fitful darts, our vision could not bear,—
Whose being we denied,—with sudden burst,
Has wrapped the country in its blaze accursed.
America is plunged in civil war.
Her very life she now is struggling for.
To save her from a death of endless shame,
Her sons, who still of sons deserve the name,
Must face her truthless and misguided sons,
With clashing sabres, and earth-jarring guns.

In other lands, or times, the bards might tell
What strifes and "moving accidents" befell,—
Might picture forth each stormy battle-scene,
And crown each hero with his laurel green;
But who shall linger on the earth so long,
That he may trace in narratory song,
And lucidly present upon his page
The war America is forced to wage?

A contest such as Earth ne'er saw before,
Must bear such fruit as contest never bore,—
Must prove the truth to every tribe and clan,
That civil liberty is safe for man.
The arid plains of far New Mexico
Must drink the blood of Union's friend and foe,
And eastward thence, to old Atlantic's beach,
Unbroken must the line of battle reach.
From Chesapeake to Rio Grande's mouth,
Along the jagged sea-coast of the South,
The thunders of the conflict must resound
And mangled human forms must fleck the ground.

X.

Unruffled never is the course of Right;
The days of darkness follow days of light.
The men who breathe America's free air,
For good or ill, will never fail to dare.
He slumbers not, by whom 'tis understood
When for the righteous cause defeat is good.
A people nobly battling for the Right,
Must learn to "walk by faith, and not by sight,"—
Must be instructed by the chastening rod,
And wait the grinding of the "Mills of God."

One day on every spirit, as it passed,
Impressed a stamp which will forever last:
It was a glorious morn; the July sun
Was breathing to our hearts a glad "Well done;"
And, as we met each other on the street,
Each visage seemed the plaudit to repeat.
Our souls were ready for an upward bound,
And soon the upward-heaving force was found;
It was a shout, a high, exultant shout
Of "Glorious Victory!" that sounded out
Upon the placid air. We do not wait
To question; with ecstatic joy elate,

We say, and say again: "Our cause is won;
What rebels could do is already done;
Their mad attempt is fully ended now,
And all to Union's majesty must bow;
Our country's safe; heroic men no more,
For her salvation, precious blood shall pour."
We hurry to and fro, such words to speak,
While ruddy joy sits blooming on each cheek;
Each eye,—But what is this? What can it mean?
Has every man a frightful spectre seen?
All lips are white; all eyes with horror stare;
Is death or madness hov'ring in the air?
This cruel truth has flashed along the street,
Consuming in our breasts a falsehood sweet:
"With headlong rush the Union soldiers fly,
And traitors lift their shouts of triumph high!"

   For them who still retain the use of sense,
Succeed two days of terrible suspense,
Until the crushing message from Bull Run
Exhausts its never-equalled power to stun.
The third day comes, and the suspense is o'er;
For rising, like the distant ocean's roar,
And hourly swelling for a mightier sweep,
The People's voice, in tones distinct and deep,
Declares that this Republic shall survive,
Though all the Devils for its ruin strive:
The readiness for temporary strife
Becomes a willingness to fight through life.

XI.

To fight! O, dark necessity of Earth,
Since wickedness in Eden had its birth!
That one should be compelled by sin to choose
The dignity of manliness to lose,
And sacred trusts ignobly to betray,
Or fellow-men in bloody death to lay!
That, for the vindication of the Right,
So many eyes should close to Heaven's light;
Such noble forms be laid in winding-sheets;
Such throngs of mourners go about the streets.

Till use had wrought a shield before our hearts,
Which checked the driving of affliction's darts,
So cruelly their bearded points did tear,
We feared the failing of our power to bear.
When Ellsworth, young, ingenuous, and brave,
With mangled breast was covered in the grave;
When brilliant Winthrop ended his career,
In presence of the foes he could not fear;
When Baker's lips of eloquence were closed,
And on the bloody sod his head reposed;
And, O, when Lyon led his brave ones on,
With glorious death heroic life to crown,

What utter impotence in language dwelt,
To give expression to the ache we felt!
O, peacefully may fallen patriots sleep;
Their honor in our "Heart of hearts" we'll keep,
And ever shall the loyal bosom swell,
When one is named who for the Union fell.

XII.

It yields assuagement of the mourner's pain,
To know that life has not been given in vain;
And tender Pity, reaching from the sky,
To stricken souls has brought that knowledge nigh.
When stern Adversity its work has done,
And needful ends of discipline were won,
The righteous Sovereign blessed the loyal brave,
And signal for the Right's advancement gave.

And now, behold, with what a lustre shine
Achievements crowned with benisons divine!
Du Pont's exultant riders of the deep,
'Twixt fort and fort in fiery circles sweep,
And raise for loyalty a voice so high,
That Treason's champions in terror fly,
And joyously, on Carolina's shore,
Ascend the stars and stripes, to fall no more.

Upon Kentucky's soil a Union band
Fierce Zollicoffer's swift assault withstand;
Assail in turn as with a lion's bound,
And lay their foemen thick upon the ground.

And now the rebel host, in scattered flocks,
Are wildly rushing to the mountain rocks.

Believing Foote moves up the Tennessee,
And soon beholds a thing which must not be:
The flag of Treason waves upon a fort,
And sternly bids him cut his voyage short.
He makes that flag the object of his aim,
And, wrapped in boiling smoke, and shooting flame,
Through iron hail, in line direct he drives,
Till traitors piteously beg their lives.

With trenches, hills, and rifle-pits around,
At Donelson are rebel thousands found;
Poor men! condemned to recognize as chief
So vile a wretch as Floyd, the perjured thief.
The degradation will not long endure,
For Grant is coming, with approaches sure.
They would escape; McClernand's in the way,
And thrice his number sternly holds at bay,
Till Smith prepares, and, with a whirlwind rush,
His brave ones all opposing foemen crush,
And Wallace gathers up a force which sweeps
The rebel remnants into panting heaps.
Then Floyd and Pillow meanly sneak away,
And rebel thousands yield at break of day;
For Grant proposes on the works to move,
And prowess of his heroes further prove.

Deep in the Western wilderness, three days,
With hostile fires the quaking hill-tops blaze,

While Curtis, Sigel, Davis prove their right
To head the Western patriots in fight.
For Union then there is a joyful shout,
And Treason mourns a mighty army's rout;
And then "Pea Ridge" becomes a name of cheer
To all who hold our country's honor dear.

   As night, and thunder, and the lightning's glare,
Suggest what Pope's grim engineers prepare,
A gust of terror from New Madrid blows
A multitude of Union's proudest foes.
At Island Ten they find but little rest;
By Pope and Foote from every quarter pressed,
They flee again, but in the dark morass,
Beneath the starry flag as captives pass.

   As over Shiloh's field the daylight breaks,
A startling shock a sleeping army wakes:
They come! they come! By myriads they pour,
With crackling musketry and cannons' roar.
Our braves leap into lines, in columns form,
And breast the fury of the sudden storm.
Outnumbered, as they sullenly retire,
There is no slack'ning of their deadly fire,
But still against the fearful odds they fight,
Till Shiloh wears the sable pall of night.
So soon as they behold again the sun,
The bloody contest is again begun;
The tide is turned, and now the foe must yield;
The Union army holds the silent field.

A tempest rages on the North State's coast,
And all a gallant, ship-imprisoned host
Is loudly threatened with a direful wreck,
While Burnside stands upon a heaving deck
And trusts in God. The tempest moves away,
And soon the patriots, in stern array,
As breezes puff along the battle-smoke,
Are seen to stand, the masters of Roanoke.

Without delay again they are afloat,
And now the Neuse gives back their bugle-note.
They disembark upon the miry bank,
And at the dawn, each in his proper rank,
And each prepared to offer up his life,
They steadily approach the place of strife.
Who would not say the mad attempt must fail
That line of frowning breastworks to assail?
But the attempt is made; the day is won;
In wild dismay ten thousand rebels run,
For Burnside, Reno, Foster, Parke have led
Such loyal men as traitors well may dread.

The time has come for Farragut to strike;
What in the past is his achievement like?
A fort is thundering on either hand,
And massive chains are stretched from land to land.
The burning rafts are ready to descend,
And iron monsters will their terrors lend.
Amid the huddled ships will gunboats dash,
And rams the solid ribs of oak will crash.

What mighty manager of words has power
To picture forth the tumult of the hour,
When Farragut was plunging on his way
Against the fury of that dread array?

   The strife was o'er; and, when the sun arose,
The Union fleet, beyond the reach of foes,
Though bruised and grimed, lay tranquilly at rest
On Mississippi's broad, unruffled breast,
Prepared to seek the Crescent City's face,
And free her from Secession's foul disgrace,—
To introduce the earnestness and skill,
The mastery of Butler's mind and will.

XIII.

It could not be forever thus; such pains
As prove to sinful men that God still reigns,
And make them know their fancied gold is dross,
Were winged abroad by unimagined loss.
When praise is stolen from the King on high,
The creatures of His hand to glorify,
'Tis needful the idolaters should see
How pitiful a worshipped man can be.

O, how resplendent was the ruddy light
Which banished all the gloom of Bull Run's night,
When young McClellan's meteoric flame
Burst forth upon our sky! To speak his name
Was then to taste a ripe and luscious joy.
McClellan! he it was who should destroy
The dragon of Rebellion, and should place
Eternity's broad seal on Freedom's base.

With joyful confidence the nation bent
Her energies to his support. She sent
By tens of myriads, to fill his ranks,
Her best beloved sons, with hearty thanks

That they were privileged, at his command,
Before infuriate rebel hosts to stand.

He showed himself a man of wondrous skill
To dress, and group, and organize, and drill.
He sat his horse with a peculiar grace,
And often spurred him, at a dashing pace,
Along the front of his parading host,
And made it seem earth ne'er before could boast
A man so formed for every warlike feat,
So grand a chief, a hero so complete.

At times, we felt that something must be wrong,
When Autumn passed, and Winter moved along,
And still that mighty army struck no blow,
Nor stirred to meet the near, and threat'ning foe.
But we were told, "The mud is very deep,
And certainly McClellan's not asleep,
But has his plans, and soon will make a move
Which plainly his pre-eminence will prove."
Unwilling to confess ourselves deceived,
We welcomed this defence, and still believed.

At length we thought our trustfulness approved;
The day arrived on which the army moved;
Then expectation sharpened every sense,
And hope shed wild'ring sweetness on suspense.
We heard of rushing on the foeman's track,
And then of marching out, and marching back.
Then came mysterious hints of wondrous schemes,

And strategy surpassing wildest dreams:
A strokes of genius would amaze the world,
And Treason down to Erebus be hurled.

   The fogs of mystery were cleared away:
In Hampton Roads a fleet of transports lay,
And with confusing hum, and splash, and roar,
A cloud of men were swarming to the shore.

   Elate with hope, and strong in purpose high,
The love of country lighting every eye,
They quickly formed in long, and deep array,
The order, "Forward," panting to obey.
The long expected hour had come at last;
The days of tedious preparation past,
Their lines invincible would now advance,
And, quickened by their chief's inspiring glance,
Assail the hostile bands that blocked their path,
And, with the vehemence of righteous wrath,
Upon the capital of Treason rush,
And once for all the horrid monster crush.

   Alas! though all the world can plainly see
That this is possible, 'tis not to be:
The chief has passed the limit of his sphere,
And honor has abandoned his career.
The nation's idol, held almost divine,
Before that peerless host begins to whine,
Because the nation's heart is not laid bare,
That he, poor quiv'ring, nerveless thing, may dare

Advance against a despicable force,
Which could not for an hour impede his course.

It is a tale to bid hot blushes rise;
A tale with pity's tears to blind the eyes;
And yet a tale admiring love to wake,
And bid all patriots fresh courage take.
If shame is felt for one's faint-heartedness,
For fruitless death of myriads, keen distress,
That army's deeds should make our bosom swell,
And ground the faith that all will yet be well.

When Williamsburg's intrenchments rose to view,
And from their fiery mouths destruction flew,
The patient valor of the bloody stand,
The steady movement of the less'ning band,
The charge impetuous of Hancock's men,
And that triumphant shout they lifted then,
Threw terrors maddening among their foes,
And made it easy, had McClellan chose,
To seize at once on Treason's central spring,
And have rebellion a departed thing.

When Chickahominy foamed on his way,
For watchful foes to isolate a prey,
The deadly falling flack at Seven Pines,
The moveless posture of the slender lines,
The stand of company against brigade,
The furious assaults at Fair Oaks made,
Procured for patriots another sight
Of rebel multitudes in headlong flight.

And now begins the memorable week,
Whose tale to far-off centuries will speak
Of valor tested in a thousand ways,
And glowing ever with intenser rays.
From Shenandoah's valley Jackson whirls,
And, like a thunderbolt, his column hurls
Upon a second isolated force.
They face him in his desolating course;
He masses here and masses there in vain;
The ground is hideous with his heaps of slain;
The harvesters of Death, through all the day,
They hold that overwhelming throng at bay.

A hurried march by night succeeds the strife,
And such becomes the Union army's life.
For food and sleep they have the might of will,
Until they plant their feet on Malvern Hill,
And there decisively the conflict close,
By hurling back the avalanche of foes
With such terrific energy that, hence,
Their dread will serve them as a sure defence.

XIV.

As thickest clouds resist approaching dawn,
The veil of hope, o'er understanding drawn,
Gave us to learn, with slowly swelling pain,
The wretched failure of the great campaign.
When rigid truth at last had claimed her own,
And all the feared became the fully known,
A strange paralysis possessed each heart.
We neither wept nor raved, but each apart,
We slowly walked, or sat with folded arms,
Untouched by hope of joys, or fear of harms,
Without a thought which human speech could serve,
Or feeling which could agitate a nerve,
And yet with thoughts and feelings so immense,
They almost burst the bond of soul and sense.

But we awoke; the future's signal-fire
Bade all the shadows of the past retire;
Our eyes were turned upon the Rapidan;
There, there already, was the rebel van;
The myriads were rushing, fired with hope
Of sweeping through the thin array of Pope,
And onward, onward still, with no delay,
Till Washington should lie their helpless prey.

The patriots well understood the state;
Each felt intrusted with a nation's fate;
Their shouts defiant through the forest broke;
The Rappahannock was embanked in smoke.
While bloody forms grew thick on either brink,
And yet the fords' defenders would not shrink.

The baffled enemies could pass around
The line they could not break. Once more they found
The Union soldiers and their deadly fire;
The slender band compelled them to retire,
And make détour again, and yet again:
O, what a question wrung our spirits then!
Could those heroic few still hold in check
That multitude, and stay the nation's wreck,
Till from the James, their brothers hastening,
A glorious deliverance should bring?

They fully did their work. Their brothers came;
And, had no chieftain clothed himself with shame,
The swift, complete redemption of Bull Run
Had then proclaimed the rebel cause undone.
But still McClellan quibbled, and deferred,
And still he gave, and still he broke his word,
Till Porter's barefaced treachery had wrought
His own, beside the ruin that he sought.

Then came the dismal days when Maryland
Beheld invasion's slimy flood expand;
And then South Mountain shook beneath the tread

Of patriots, before whom traitors fled.
Up, up they charged, along the rugged steep:
The cannons roared, but hindered not their sweep;
Before their bayonets the lines gave way;
The pinnacle was theirs and theirs the day.
On that high spot the banner floated out;
And far-off hills gave back the greeting shout.

Three days had passed, when face to face, once more,
The armies stood, each stronger than before.
'Twas Hooker's province, stationed at the right,
With his tried columns to commence the fight;
Though shortly he was carried from the field,
He saw the stubborn foe begin to yield.
Then Sumner came, with silver-waving hair,
A voice to cheer, a noble heart to dare.
But thick upon his front the rebels massed;
On every side his men were falling fast;
His shattered ranks were slowly giving ground,
When Franklin's heroes, with a sudden bound,
And wild, defiant cheer, were at their side,
And, in an instant, turned the battle's tide.

Down at the left, beneath a batt'ried ridge,
The corps of Burnside stormed a narrow bridge,
Then upward pressed, and struggled on, till night
Forbade the further progress of the fight.
The dawn was watched by many eager eyes,
And many hearts were lifted to the skies,
In thanks, and adoration, for the hour

Which placed rebellion in the patriot's power.
Alas! McClellan thought it best to wait,
And at another dawn it was too late.

   Kentucky soon our chief attention claimed;
While treason-goaded children scourged, and shamed,
The robbing bands that Smith and Morgan led,
Like swarming vampires, on her life-blood fed.
And then, alas! the bearer of a trust
That should exalt, preferred to lick the dust.
The fear, that Slavery would experience harm,
Froze Buell's heart, and paralyzed his arm.
Instead of pressing up the Tennessee,
And setting all the mountain region free,
He followed in the rebel army's wake,
As if to see what course it meant to take,
Till Bragg had learned, upon Ohio's brink,
There were such foes as gave him cause to shrink.
And when the swelling of the Union force
Had made it possible to end the course
Of that invading army, Buell still
For Slavery trembled; and at Perryville
McCook and his companions, left alone,
With valor unexceeded vainly shone.

   There came a change,—a Union chief was found,
Whom no such despicable fetters bound;
A new directing spirit soon disclosed
Of what true stuff that army was composed.

Amid immovably established claims
To high renown, that of the coupled names
Of Murfreesboro and of Rosecrans
Shall stand the sweep of fate, the shock of chance.

XV.

In these our days there is a power abroad
Whose tests hypocrisy cannot defraud,
Which modest diffidence cannot evade,
Which wrings from men the stuff whereof they're made.
And there have been disclosures that should move
Our soul's recesses in their depths, and prove
What is our admiration's utmost reach,—
What love to man is possible for each.

Throughout the North, in stations low and high,
Has gleamed a virtue worthy of the sky;
But O, the heart must swell, the lips be dumb,
When Southern patriots before us come,
The offers of pre-eminence to scorn,
Unmoved to hear the tools of treason warn;
The Reign of Terror tranquilly to brave,
And look unblenching at the opening grave;
Or penniless, from wealth and power to flee,
That still the soul from blackness may be free;
These things to do, is to present a claim
To universal love and deathless fame.
Heroic Johnson! Brownlow! Hamilton!
Eternal is the glory ye have won;

And thousands of your like, who ne'er on earth
Will find a recognition of their worth,
On heavenly plains shall stand, in robes of light,
Among the highest martyrs for the Right.

Beyond the ocean have emerged to view
The signs of manhood incorrupt and true.
A throng of needy artisans attend,
While orators their highest efforts bend,
To prove the term will come of their sore need,
When traitors in America succeed;
But they inquire: "In case of such success,
Would Slavery's power be greater, or be less?"
The orators must redden and concede
'Tis Slavery's villany for which they plead;
Or, if the hateful fact they still deny,
Their manner shows that knowingly they lie.
Then speak the artisans: "We'll hear no more;
In other ears your slimy poison pour;
By gaunt Starvation's hand we will expire,
Ere we will breathe, or cherish a desire
That they may be triumphant who rebel,
To bind their country in the chains of Hell!"

Now from that picture turn to look on this,
And change your plaudits to a scathing hiss:
The merchants and the money-changers sit
In conclave, and each face with joy is lit,
As they repeat: "America is dead
If but the traitors' hopes be duly fed;

We'll cheer them on with expectations high,
Till North and South in common ruin lie;
The hated rivalry will then be o'er,
And streams of trade for us alone will pour."
By words like these, by every grin they say
They are prepared, for an assassin's pay,
To bring on thirty millions of their race,
And generations yet to take their place,
The wretchedness, and guilt, and woe,
Which mark a mighty nation's overthrow.

And now the lordlings and their toadies see;
Oh, how they rub their little hands in glee!
In every breast a baby-joy is nursed,
Because they fancy that the " Bubble's burst."
It was a dreadful thing to think about,
When the Republic seemed so hale and stout;
'Twas greatly to be feared that all the world
In topsy-turvy jumble would be whirled,
And this atrocious principle find place,
That all mankind are of the human race.
And then no more a little vicious dunce,
Whose family was justly honored once,
Would be permitted, as a crouching cur,
To treat a hero, or philosopher;
But this assault upon the Union's life,
These welcome scenes of fratricidal strife,
Allay the fear that, over all the earth,
Men will be held at what themselves are worth.

But here; what men are these? By birth they stand
As citizens of this afflicted land,
And far from Slavery's soul-polluting air,
They reaped the blessings of parental care.
The truth was shown them in ten thousand lights,
That human beings all have sacred rights;
And yet, since first the fearful strife began,
To save the Government that honors man,
They have revealed the union of their hearts
With Slavery's lords, whose secret, fiendish arts,
A tyranny on freedom's wreck to raise,
Now show their fruits in war's appalling blaze.

When patriots victoriously fight,
And loyal hearts are swelling with delight,
In look and tone ill-natured, crabbed, cross,
They talk of nothing but the "frightful loss;"
But when the traitors their successes win,
The trouble is in keeping down a grin;
While gladness sparkles in their snaky eyes,
They set their lungs at heaving long-drawn sighs,
And speak to every man upon the street
About the "crushing, terrible defeat."
With not a word of censure for our foes,
They harp incessantly upon the woes
Which in the train of war the land befall,
And charge on Northern men the blame for all.
The Government for every act they curse,
And hold that Satan's reign could not be worse.
The President, to save the nation's life,

Will let oppression perish in the strife,
And sooty Africans in arms will see,
That white Americans may still be free;
He therefore is the object of their hate,
A monster, tyrant, fool, and reprobate.
When but a portion of the power he wields
The Constitution for the crisis yields,
And 'tis not safe in treason to engage,
Oh! how these worshippers of slavery rage.
"A blow is struck at liberty," they cry;
"We'll not endure it; we'll be free or die."
Made senseless by their hated of the Right,
Against the facts that glow in noonday light,
They swear that now, all over this free land,
Grim Tyranny has stretched his iron hand.
Their orators with boundless license screech
About "Departed liberty of speech,"
Too mad to see, what meets the dullest eye,
That all such ranting gives itself the lie.

Now that America has bought with blood
The power to stem Secession's roaring flood,—
Now that she numbers with her martyred ones
Three hundred thousand of her noblest sons,
And need but make one earnest effort more,
To strike gigantic treason to the core,
And gain a footing on the solid rock
That gives no token of the mightiest shock,
These men, quite frantic at so near a view
Of that result implored by all the true,

With deafening clamors, are demanding peace,
Well knowing that, if now the contest cease,
Their country's foes will have unbounded sway,
And all her friends must slavishly obey.

   To give a color to their deeds of shame,
Of "Democrat" they steal the honored name.
The men whom traitor-hating Jackson's frown
To quiv'ring suppliants would wither down;
Who treat those truths with scoffing, and despite,
Which dying Douglas uttered for the Right;
Who fain with poisoned arrows would transfix
Such men as Butler, Stanton, Holt, and Dix,
And would rejoice to lay beneath the sod
All men like Dickinson, and Brough, and Tod;
Who are opposing with their utmost might
The myriads of Democrats who fight,
That true Democracy may live on earth
Till all mankind shall understand its worth,—
These are the Democrats! O, are there fools
Whom that high name can make their supple tools?

   What would these men? What is their real aim?
The passions of the base they would inflame,
The ignorant mislead with specious lies,
And thus procure a traitor force to rise,
And governmental power annihilate
Within the borders of each loyal State;
To save the rebel chiefs from overthrow,
They would have Northern blood in torrents flow;

This dire alternative they would present,—
To see the downfall of the Government,
And bid the traitors work their hellish will
Or all the North with scenes of carnage fill.
No baseness wears for them too foul a face,
But, with a hot affection, they embrace
Whatever with their final aim accords,
To be the lickspittles of Southern lords.

XVI.

My countrymen! shall villany prevail?
In this dread strife shall the Republic fail?
Shall perjured murderers, triumphant, reign
O'er all our loved America's domain?
Shall we acknowledge them our rightful lords,
And watch with trembling for their lightest words?
Shall Liberty forsake our conquered land,
And Slavery's night on every side expand?
Shall wrong, descending from the mount of power,
With widening sweep flow on from hour to hour,
Till all the land beneath its waves shall lie,
And men shall cease to dream of aught that's high?
Shall it be said, in ages yet to be,
"The peoples of the earth might now be free,
Had Northern men, in that decisive day,
Not basely thrown their manliness away?"

O, blessed be thy name, Eternal God!
Though hard to bear is thy correcting rod,
We yet may hope that from the Throne above
The fruits will fall of Thy paternal love.
That spirit which heroic aims imparts,
Is mightily at work in human hearts,

And steadily, as heavenly orbs revolve,
Extends and grows in strength the high resolve,
Whate'er the cost, whate'er the certain pain,
The Union, in its wholeness, to maintain;
While plaintive moans and sharp, distressful cries
From all the regions of Rebellion rise,
Betokening a fearful day at hand,
When traitor-chiefs as criminals shall stand,
With all the blackness of their souls in view,
Before the men who once believed them true.

O, who will let the golden hours go by,
And opportunities forever fly,
In this stupendous work to bear a part,
And wake a deathless songster in his heart?
O, let our souls the bands of slumber break,
And of our privilege the measure take;
A crisis all momentous to mankind
Invites the energy of every mind,
And bids affection, with its richest glow,
From all the fountains of the spirit flow.
To countless millions will this contest seal
A wretched fate, or everlasting weal.

Disciples of the Crucified! Behold
Oppression striding on, with visage bold,
Your Master's Gospel underfoot to tread,
And crush the truths on which your souls have fed.
O, all ye men, and women who would grieve
If truth and righteousness this world should leave;

All ye who prize the welfare of your race;
All ye who recognize a God of grace;
Put forth your power, and lift your prayers on high,
Till treason, vanquished, from the land shall fly.

LIBERTY'S ORDEAL.

PART SECOND.

Part Second.

I.

'Tis Independence Day in 'Sixty-three;
The fields are basking in a tranquil sea
Of golden light.   Sweet silence has control :
All nature's wooing to repose of soul.
And yet our souls repose not, but a strange
Commingling, and a rapid, ceaseless change
Of thoughts and heart-stirs set at naught the force
Which erst could flow with unobstructed course.

July the Fourth! our nation's day of days!
The name pronounced, emerging from the haze
Of generations gone, all glowing, stand
In Independence Hall the peerless band.
The Declaration bears the name of each,
And thoughts, which know the impotence of speech,
On massive brows present their swelling lines,
And kindle in all eyes their blazing signs.
One face reveals the joy from visions caught
Of weal for men of distant ages bought;

Here, braced and nerved, is one who sees the hour
Of final strife with haughty Britain's power;
Those eyes reveal, by their unearthly light,
A soul reposing on celestial might;
And all stand forth with that heroic mien,—
That majesty—which only then is seen,
When men are wholly offered for the Right,
And fortune, life, and sacred honor plight.

O, Independence! Gushing from that word,
Is music sweet as mortal ever heard.
America, cut loose from all the clogs,
And bursting from the dank and stifling fogs
Of senseless forms, stupidities revered,
And customs worshipped though with guilt besmeared!
No more at privilege of rank to cower,
Or tremble at the balancing of power,
But independent on her way to move,
Inviting each his proper worth to prove,
And making sure to truth and righteousness
The free unfolding of their power to bless!

May not her glory soon become a shame,
And Independence a derided name?
So they believe, who, with malignant eyes,
Have seen the fabric of her greatness rise.
With shouts of exultation, they behold
The gory tide of battle northward rolled,
And in the vales of Pennsylvania see
The ruthless ravage of the hordes of Lee.

Their fancies hurry on, to name the day
When Washington will own the rebel sway,
And all the foes of Liberty will cry,
"So shamefully let all republics die."

   May not the ground be firm on which they build?
May not their hopes be speedily fulfilled?
O no! O, righteous heavenly Father, no!
Thou wilt not crush mankind with such a blow.
The fate is merited, but Thou'lt forbear;
O, Thou art merciful, and Thou wilt spare.

II.

Alone, with anxious brow, the President
Observes the opening door. His eyes are bent
Upon a missive brought; he turns away,
And something says, "The comer must not stay."
O, let the broad breast heave, and waters rise
From heart-recess, to cool the burning eyes.
Composure comes, and peace unknown before,
For, while he reads the missive o'er, and o'er,
A spirit seems, in whisperings, to tell
That near the mighty river all is well.

A joyful purpose gleams in Lincoln's eyes—
"Yes, yes," he says, "before a moment flies,
This peace of soul with lightning-speed must flow,
That millions may its heavenly sweetness know."
And now he speaks to us of condolence
For gallant ones laid low in our defence;
And now, in tones subdued, a truth imparts,
Which wakes to hope serene our softened hearts;
Then points our spirits to the Throne above,
And bids us ne'er forget the Father's love.

His vision seems to catch unearthly power,
Each word he speaks so well befits the hour.
We're on the field of Gettysburg. Behold
The shroud of smoke above the mountain rolled,
And, deluged with the cloudless noonday's light,
The ground which felt the surgings of the fight.
For condolence this is the hour indeed ;
O, here the heart of adamant might bleed !
Before you, on the left, and on the right,
To utmost limit of defining sight,
Mid fallen steeds, and caissons overthrown,
And flags, and guns, in wild disorder strown,
The prostrate bodies of your brothers slain
Resistlessly your aching eyes enchain.

Here, at your feet, upon his side is cast
A youthful father. When he breathed his last
His arm was curved, as if it fondly pressed
The bright-eyed prattler to his manly breast.

There lies a boy, as if he rested now
That head with glossy curls, and marble brow,
Upon a mother's lap, and gave his soul,
In dreamy bliss, to love's benign control.

And there's a strong-framed youth, whose visage-lines
Of thought and daring are the patent signs;
A youth to plan, and plans to carry out;
A youth whom one could lean upon, no doubt.
When, but a moment since, his spirit fled,
" My parents will be childless now," he said.

O, see that death-grasp on the picture there!
It is a maiden.   She is passing fair.
Ah! weep, poor girl, weep till your eyes are dim;
It would be wicked not to mourn for him.

But there, beyond!   O, what a heavenly light
That visage caught before the spirit's flight!
You bend your steps among the dead, and look;
Beside his face there lies an open book,
And, where the bloody finger-traces lead,
"Let not your heart be troubled," you can read.

As now your vision sweeps the field again,
Your heart is saying: "Thus my fellow-men,
On these declivities, and o'er that plain,
Are thickly lying, mercilessly slain.
O God! Thy balm for wounded hearts prepare,
For cruelly the rooted ties must tear
When souls they cling to can no longer stay,
But with a start so sudden burst away.
Around the gray-haired parent cast Thine arm;
The widow, and the orphan, shield from harm;
On sister, and affianced maid, bestow
The peace which Thou alone canst make to flow."

Condoling thus, and passing round the hill,
New scenes your heart with new emotions fill.
Here prostrate forms, though not bereft of life,
Are thickly gathered from the place of strife.
The smiles of fortitude the sufferers wear

But poorly help the spectacle to bear;
Each bleeding brow, and shattered limb can smite
Your inmost being with a giant's might.

You turn, from these distressful sights to shrink,
But then of manhood's high requirements think,
And soon in deeds your pity finds relief,
And active love is sweetening your grief;
With energy you never knew before
You work, and work, till you can work no more.

A tree, which crowns the summit of a hill,
Lets fall a cooling shade from branches still,
While you recline there with a heart at ease,
And whisper to yourself in words like these:
" 'Tis dark enough, and yet not wholly dark;
The train of war some spots of brightness mark;
To make no mention of the noble zeal
Which proffers life for the Republic's weal,
Nor yet to speak of traits that spring to light
Amid the roar, and crashing of the fight,
What I have witnessed in those wounded men
Has brought such nobleness within my ken,
That I shall henceforth discipline my mind
To think more hopefully of all my kind,
And nevermore a doubt will entertain
That lands may prosper where no monarchs reign.
Such thoughtlessness of self! such words of love
To friends at home, and Him who rules above!
Such quenchless ardor in the Union's cause,

And loyal reverence for her righteous laws!
The brightness there, until my latest day,
Will cast a mellow cheer along my way.

"And then, what gain that I can justly prize
Those angel women, with their tender eyes!
So lovingly they gave the cordials out;
With such a gentle swiftness moved about;
Each need their eyes so readily discerned;
Relief so quickly came where'er they turned;
Their presence caused such thankful smiles to rise,
I almost thought them natives of the skies.
And I remember now that everywhere
I've seen the proofs of loyal woman's care
For those who come, the fiery storms to breast,
That once again their country may have rest."

III.

AMID these thoughts you hear a sudden rush,
And horsemen, bursting through the underbrush,
Are at your side, and swinging to the ground,
And one exclaims, as, with a forward bound,
He gathers all the prospect in his eyes,
"Yes; here the field in all its glory lies.
O, here's the spot where Treason got the blow
Which laid her hopes and high pretensions low.

"Far onward, at the left, that wooded height
Was honored with the opening of the fight.
There Wadsworth found the rebels in his way,
And, with a zeal which could not brook delay,
He bade his guns and musketry begin
Their judgment-call, and treason-dooming din.
And there rode out, upon that open space,
A soldier peerless for his manly grace.
'Twas Wadsworth's chief; 'twas Reynolds, with that eye,
Which, better than another's, could descry
The ground where patriots might firmest stand,
And best their country's thunderbolts command.
But O, that bearing high! It showed the foe
Where Freedom could receive the direst blow:

A hundred rifles moved at Slavery's will,
And Reynolds lay there motionless, and still.

"But Wadsworth faltered not, and Doubleday,
Directing then the patriot array,
Brought forces to his left, while Robinson,
Upon his right, a gallant band led on.
They pressed against the storm, until they stood
There, at the upper margin of the wood.
'This hill,' said they, 'is better than the plain:
Here will we stand; here best we shall remain.'
And there they did remain for glorious hours,
And seemed endowed with superhuman powers,
Against that host to make their purpose good:
Shock after shock, they stubbornly withstood,
Till Howard's corps, at length, came rushing down
Upon their right there, straight beyond the town.

"In those men's ears was ringing then a name
Which marks the soldier for consuming shame;
And, when they heard the uproar of the fight,
Their eyes were kindled with a fierce delight.
They reached the spot assigned, and formed, and dressed,
With muscles braced, knit brows, and lips compressed—
Disgrace was changed to glory. Nevermore
Shall blushes rise for the Eleventh Corps—
With twice their number, like a raging flood,
Came Ewell's madmen, panting for their blood.
With bayonets in poise they rushed, and yelled;
But like a wall their ground the patriots held.

The masters of the wrath with which they flamed,
They loaded swiftly, and they surely aimed.
The fierce assailants stumbled o'er their dead;
They looked; they turned; in wild confusion fled.
Again their line was formed, and forward moved—
Vain, as before, the furious onslaught proved.

"But now the sun was low, and Howard said,
'Most gallantly, my heroes, you have led
In this great conflict; but I plainly see
That night is in advance of victory,
For Providence has singled out this field
Of Freedom's fate a prophecy to yield.
We'll choose a place then for to-morrow's fight,
With ample room, upon our left, and right,
For all our brothers, who with eager haste
Are asking where the traitors may be faced.'

"While thick around the deadly missiles flew,
With steadiness the patriots withdrew,
And seized, according to the wise design,
The centre of this ridgy crescent line.
The twilight soon was gone, and well content
With all the lot which Providence had sent;
Self-praise, and hope assured in every breast,
Beneath the smiling stars we courted rest.
It was a valor-breathing sleep we slept:
As through our joints the grateful stupor crept,
Our drowsy sense was of the rumbling wheel,
Of tramping myriads, and of clatt'ring steel,

With here and there a low, decisive voice;
And dreams of growing power made us rejoice
Through all that night.

———"At morn we looked around,
And facts more cheering than our visions found:
Along that farthest ridge, upon our right
Were Slocum's thousands, marshalled for the fight.
Next on his left was Newton's corps arrayed;
Then Howard's proud battalions were displayed;
And next was Hancock's portion of the field;
And farther still acclaims of greeting pealed
As Sickles passed along his threat'ning line;
And still beyond, where trees the view confine,
The veterans of Sykes, with practised eyes,
Were watching for the battle-signs to rise.
On every height, commanding each ravine,
The brazen ministers of death were seen,
Their crushing globes made ready at their sides,
And guided for the strife their stalwart guides.

"We waited for the onset, till the sun
His journey from the summit had begun;
But still it was delayed. At times the sound
Of musketry would draw our gaze around
To left or right, then stillness would ensue.
At length a jet of smoke! A challenge flew
Above the town, and over Hancock's men,
Who stood with Howard's near those grave-stones then.
As quick as thought, O, what a tempest broke!

All Cemetery Hill was wrapped in smoke
That rolled out blood-hue from the flash on flash,
And quaked, with unremitting roar and crash,
While shrieked the flying, burst the fallen shell,
And all around our gallant soldiers fell.

"That storm raged on two hours—just at its close,
Emerging from that western wood, our foes
Approached our left,—a dark, portentous cloud,—
Mass after mass, with furious mien they crowd.
Along their front the smoke begins to pour.
The crackling sound becomes a ceaseless roar.
Now Sickles faces them; rage answers rage;
But too unequal is the strife we wage.
Alas! our heroes are compelled to yield,
And Sickles must be carried from the field.
On rush the foe, with yells that fill the air;
But Meade is near us; Meade is everywhere:
The band of Sykes are brought up from the left,
And leap with joy into the fiery cleft,
And Hancock's patriots, plunging from the right,
Make more terrific, the terrific fight.
But rebel columns still on columns press;
Though thousands fall, their number seems no less;
From Newton's line Meade hurries down a force;
But this does not undam the battle's course.

"You should have seen the sight which I saw then:
'Twas Sedgwick, with his weary, foot-sore men.
A day and night, and yet another day,

Those heroes have been hastening on their way.
They see how stands the undecided fight;
Their eyes blaze up with patriotic light;
'Thank God! Thank God!' they cry, 'we're not too late;'
Their knapsacks drop; for Sedgwick's voice they wait;
'Go forward now!' he shouts, and on they rush;
They reach the foe; the bristling line they crush;
The day is ours; the matchless battle's won;
Across the plain the routed rebels run.

"Our shouts were sounding still, when, at the right,
We heard the tumult of another fight.
The line of Howard Ewell's men assailed,
To madness wrought since Hill and Longstreet failed.
They swept our forces from that forward knoll,
And down the slope the flood began to roll.
It was the vale of death to which they pressed;
Our men had formed upon the other crest;
And now in ghastly swaths the rebels fell
Before the storm of canister and shell.
More furious grew the tempest; Newton sprang
To Slocum's aid; the call of Hancock rang
Once more, and higher still our hearts were strung,
Till back the decimated foe was flung.

"Then all was still; the wearied armies slept,
And Pity o'er the field her vigil kept,
Bewailing, hour on hour, the wickedness
Which poured that whelming deluge of distress.

"But, soon as morning o'er the hill-tops broke,
With strength renewed, the battle-spirit woke;
Where last the fight had ceased, it opened first;
At once along the front of Slocum burst,
In smoke and flame of thund'rous cannonade,
The anger of America betrayed.
And then at once, with wild, demoniac yell,
Like raving legions vomited from hell,
Impelled by rage, and ruled by no design,
The foe sprang up, and charged our blazing line.
Heroic firmness, reckless fury met;
As flints the patriots their faces set;
Unflinchingly they breasted, six long hours,
The desp'rate charges, and the leaden showers,
Then made one dash upon the dense array,
And swept it as a thing of naught away.

"A period followed of expectant rest;
The rebel leaders, baffled and distressed,
Were forced to think such thoughts as made them quail;
Their self-deluding power began to fail;
Hurled back at every onset from the field,
They heard the frightful question, 'Must we yield?
O, what a fall from that self-glorious height,
At which they caught the prospect of the fight!
Not, after all, to capture Washington,
And thither bring their great dictator on?
To nothingness behold the vision fade
Of European, and of Northern aid?

Give up ambitious hopes, and, mid the wrecks,
Continue fighting but to save their necks?

"Such questionings no fruit but madness bear.
With all the energy of fell despair,
Their batteries in one thick mass they threw
Before our central line, and missiles flew,
With horrid screechings, wildly overhead,
While others ploughed those chambers of the dead,
And others cut broad paths among our men.
No words can picture what we witnessed then:
Our horses fell; our guns were overthrown;
The wrecks of caissons at the heavens were blown;
Our other guns, to tenfold fury wrought,
Like ministers of boundless wrath were fought;
They breathed out heaving clouds of fire and smoke,
And awful was the voice with which they spoke.

"At length there is a lull, and we behold
The surging masses through the woodland rolled.
Straight at the Cemetery Hill they dash;
The shrill-toned musketry begins to crash;
They struggle onward; now they're beaten back,
With corpses thickly strewn along their track.
But pressing from behind are myriads more,
And on they come, more reckless than before;
Great gaps along the nearing front are cleft;
And filled from the exhaustless number left.
Their rifles levelled at our cannoneers,
The hill they mount with loud, exultant cheers.

Alas! all guns but Cowan's six are dumb,
And these they near,—with rapid strides they come;
'Pour in the canister!' the Captain cries;
From all the brazen throats the volley flies,
And limbless, headless trunks a barrier form
Too hideous for human foes to storm.
'They're ours!' Webb shouts, and with a sudden bound
We swoop the captive thousands from the ground.

"The battle ended there. Their guns awhile
Snarled out denial, in the rebel style,
But soon confessed defeat, and slunk away;
And now, this glorious Independence Day,
The panic-stricken host are fleeing fast
Along the vales they late so proudly passed,
While, hanging on their rear, and straggling flanks,
Our cavalry pluck thousands from their ranks."

O, friends, did not the President say well,
Our hearts with grateful reverence should swell?
A moment leave the heaven-provided scene,
And look upon the things that might have been:
The Union army crushed; the victory
Of Freedom's foes complete; the traitors free
To work their will,—destroying rage to pour
On Philadelphia, or on Baltimore;
The nation's capital beneath their feet,
And there erected Treason's central seat;
Oppression's Northern lovers undisguised,
And all the timid loyal paralyzed;

In Europe sounding the exultant roar,
"Rejoice! the Great Republic is no more."
O, shall we ever cease that God to praise,
Who, in the hearts of patriots, did raise
The moveless barrier which stopped the flow
Of such a desolating tide of woe?

IV.

Nor here alone, this glorious day, expand
The rays of heavenly favor on our land.
Another rebel army, in dismay,
With all that hinders flight bestrew the way,
Regardful, in their headlong course, of naught
But distance from the Helena they sought.
Once more to failure foolish Price has led,
And lips are cursing now his hoary head
Which, yesterday, were clam'rous with the vaunt
Of shutting off the stream of life from Grant.
In Prentiss, and his men, the spirit stirred,
And now their shouts of victory are heard.

But here, behold! Is this a real sight?
The Union banner waving o'er that height?
In Vicksburg's heart that column clad in blue?—
Those patriotic shouts? O, is it true?
This too the gracious Father lets us see,
On Independence Day, in 'sixty-three.
The mighty stronghold, where resounded first,
O'er Mississippi's tide, the voice accursed,
Which bade the gentle flow of commerce cease,
And war's alarms displace the joys of peace;

Whose batt'ried face so long, with horrid frown,
Has looked upon the wat'ry mirror down;
Whose thick embankments, from their stations high,
Have seemed the earth and heavens to defy;
On which all traitor-hearts their hopes have stayed;
On which responsibility was laid,
The central tract of Slavery's realm to keep
Secure from Freedom's life-imparting sweep,—
That stronghold now is held by loyal men,
And ne'er shall own Secession's rule again.

'Tis Logan's boon the banner first to plant;
But all rejoice alike—Victorious Grant
Serenely smiles. McPherson, Sherman, Blair,
And Steel, and Ord, and Osterhaus are there,
With many equals, tasting the delight
Of faith heroic changed at last to sight.
The leaders move among their noble bands,
And read in moistened eyes, and waving hands,
The love which men in fearful trials learn,
And which their hearts abundantly return.

In social groups they cluster everywhere,
For each his overflowing joy would share.
The past, they knew so lavish of distress,
Returns to-day, unstintingly to bless.
The stages of the matchless enterprise
All vividly in quick succession rise:
The dauntless ardor of the first assault,
By Nature foiled, and not through Sherman's fault;

The proof that new attacks in front were rash;
The brilliant triumph by a backward dash;
Experiment of this and that resource,
To tempt the mighty river from his course;
The fruitless arts, by bayou, pass, and lake,
Around the rugged steeps a path to break;
The readiness of brethren of the wave
The thunders of the batteries to brave;
The southward march; the crossing of the flood;
Port Gibson won with freely offered blood;
The daring sev'rance from the river-base;
Excitement of the battle-checkered chase;
The dash on Jackson, and the rapid whirl,
The battle-tempest westwardly to hurl;
The val'rous deeds at Edward's Dépôt done;
The traits displayed when Champion's Hill was won;
The driving of the rebels to their den;
The noble flood saluted once again;
The fierce assaults; the mines, and countermines;
The slow contraction of the doomful lines—
All these return, inviting joyful speech,
And eloquence to-day's the gift of each.

 And here the consummation is at last;
The harvest garnered; all the labor past.
These fastnesses, with all their grim array,
From Treason's ruthless grasp are snatched away;
And thirty thousand men in durance stand,
The vanquished foemen of their native land.

Rejoice, heroic patriots, rejoice!
And give your thankful exultation voice;
For millions wait to lift the high acclaim,
And marshal you to courts of deathless fame.

V.

That day of wonders led a shining train,
Which proved that hearts o'erjoyed new joy could gain.
But five times had the earth revolved when Banks,
For conqu'ring valor, gave his heroes thanks.
Port Hudson ours! The Mississippi free,
From farthest spring to union with the sea!
The badge of Treason from his presence hurled,
And in its place the starry flag unfurled!
Didst thou not leap, old River, at the sight,
And feel a flash of infinite delight
Along thy continent-embracing course?
'Twas hellish on thy loyal breast to force
The traitor's office. That abasement's o'er;
To thine America thou canst once more
Be true henceforth; on thy majestic tide,
With none to stay, shall her defenders ride,
And thou shalt feel her blessed spirit go
In even pace with thine eternal flow,
Dissolving chains, and breathing heavenly fire, .
And lovingly exhorting, "Go up higher."

The cup was not yet full—'Twas ours to hear
Of victories the treason-cradle near;

The forts of Charleston earnest Gillmore faced,
In stern array his dreadful engines placed.
Not swift his march, but like approach of doom,
And mortal foes could not deny him room :
Brief time their Gregg and Wagner could they keep;
And Sumter lay a traitor-warning heap.

John Morgan started gayly on a ride,
To steal some clothes, and humble Northern pride;
But found full soon that he was not the one
To do such deeds as Grierson had done,
And also learned the people of the land
Did not approve the ride which he had planned.
And, when it took such unexpected shape,
This way, and that, he bounded to escape ;
But all in vain he dodged, and skulked, and fought:
Himself and his four thousand men were caught.
Ohio's soil, as prisoners, they trod,
And Shackleford rode onward thanking God.

Then came a victory with no alloy
To tinge the gushing current of its joy.
A day of ecstasy in Tennessee!
The cruelly enslaved at last are free.
In multitudes they pour along the way;
They shout, they weep, in broken voice they pray
That Heaven may send the fulness of its bliss,
On them that bring deliverance like this.
A noble State is nobly freed at last,
And Treason from her mountain chains is cast.

A frantic frame the traitors fitly show,
Compelled the overwhelming facts to know;—
At Knoxville Burnside unrestrained commands;
And Rosecrans in Chattanooga stands.
Their chieftain, skilled in coupling oaths with lies,
Profusely swears he'll snatch again the prize.
'Tis sadly true he may cause blood to flow,
And thus increase his treasury of woe;
But, thanks to God, the soil of Tennessee
From his accursed tyranny is free.

   Amid the days that with such radiance shone,
A day of blackest infamy was thrown:
The Empire City made the foul display
Of Treason's demon-multiplying sway.
Her traitor-chiefs had diligently wrought
To aid the foes her patriots had fought.
While these were bleeding on the battle-field,
Their loved, imperilled Government to shield,
That very moment, at the hands of those,
That Government received the fellest blows.
Incessantly the *News, Express,* and *World*
Envenomed weapons at her vitals hurled.
In spacious halls, and grog-shops underground,
Secession's frantic orators were found;
And—shame of shames!—on Independence Day
A Governor was joined to their array.
The fruit was ripened soon; the tree was known,
And Northern treason to the world was shown.

I will not paint it. Hideous sight, begone!
Too deep already are thy features drawn
In every memory. A raving crowd,
With bloody hands, and imprecations loud,
Around an Orphan Home, shall henceforth rise
At mention of the men who sympathize
With braver traitors, and emblazoned there—
" 'Tis this, Americans, that we prepare."

    Far more than weapons, and strong-sinewed arms,
These men contribute for their country's harms:
Their words to her embattled foemen fly,
Reviving hopes just on the point to die,
Resolves confirming still the war to wage,
And reawaking treasonable rage;
While Union soldiers feel that all in vain
They volunteer to lie among the slain.

VI.

'Tis thus that ceaselessly to Freedom's foes
A tide of power across the ocean flows.
No frowning Alabamas could be sent
So potent as the hopeful courage lent.
O, Englishmen! we did not look for this.
When we beheld the horrible abyss
Yawn at our feet, and heard from the Most High
The summons, " Ye who would regard the cry
Of millions plunged in curable distress,
And ye who heed the rules of righteousness,
Now save your country from an overthrow
Unmatched on earth in wickedness and woe,"
And when that call we purposed to obey,
And on the sacred altar all to lay,
We thought one other people lived on earth
Which would appreciate the off'ring's worth.
O, could you know how in these latter days
Our thoughts had channelled out their fav'rite ways;
How gladly we believed forever gone
The enmity from old dissensions drawn;
With what delight we dwelt upon the ties
Unnumbered which from boons in common rise,

And of a future dreamed, when firmly bound
America and Britain would be found,
With Freedom's banner lifted and unfurled,
Confronting all the despots of the world,
You would not think our indignation strange
On waking to the vision's horrid change.

Ere yet one blow upon our country fell,
You rushed exultantly to ring her knell;
Your government, with unexampled haste,
A band of traitors on her level placed;
Your moulders of opinion, far and near,
Bade you the champions of Slavery cheer;
Your venal *Times*, intent the course to know
Where passion's overwhelming tide would flow,
And glad to find it on the side of wrong,
With frantic gestures marshalled it along;
Your demagogues the rare occasion caught,
And by maligning us your favor bought.
The motives we unbosomed at the Throne,
Where all the secrets of all hearts are known,
With full assurance that the smile divine
Along our path of sacrifice would shine,
We saw impugned as frivolous, and base,
Unfit in human hearts to hold a place.

Might not these things impel us to the view
That all your high pretensions were untrue?—
A windy sham the antislavery zeal
And broad good-will which you professed to feel?

Had we not seeming reason to declare
That Englishmen too low a manhood share,
The loves and purposes to understand
Which animate the loyal of our land?
And, when our countrymen by thousands fell
For England's sanction of the cause of hell,
Was there no provocation to the threat,
That swift revenge should wipe away the debt?

 And yet the hasty words we hasten to recall.
Committed with the right to stand or fall,
And having, from the King Supreme, in trust
To teach the world a people can be just,
'Tis only at imperial Duty's voice
That war's calamities can be our choice.
And God forbid that punishment should fall,
For guilt of many, on the heads of all.
May all remembrance cease ere we forget
The sons of Britain who have nobly set
Their matchless powers against the noisy tide
Which Slavery's heartless sympathizers ride.
The lying *Times*, and venomous *Reviews*,
Shall make us fitly prize the *Star* and *News*.
The injured millions, who, if not deceived
By faithless guides, implicitly believed,
Their prayers importunate our cause would give,
Shall be our brothers while on earth we live.
For titled ones, who wish our country's weal,
Profound respect and gratitude we feel.
As daily at the mercy-seat we bend,

Our prayers go up that blessings may descend
For Britain's Queen, whose purity of heart
Secures her sympathy to Freedom's part.

   And they who honor us with fiendish hate,
Because we hold, that, whether small or great,
A human being, in Jehovah's sight,
To upward courses has a deathless right,
May be resigned to Retribution's sweep,
Whose all-beholding eyes are strange to sleep.
The day speeds on when England will permit
No bodied baseness on her heights to sit.
Unrestingly the truth which we maintain
In British minds will widen its domain,
Till all the scaffoldings of scornful birth
Shall fall before the majesty of worth.
By this consoling faith our anger cured,
Of future union for the Right assured,
We lift our eyes from all the wrongs they see,
And hail with joy the England that shall be.

VII.

AND what of France? There is no living France.
She lies, not dead indeed, but in a trance.
What hidden thoughts and wishes may be hers,
We cannot know—she speaks no word, nor stirs.
How sad has been her lot! There was a day
When all her manacles were cast away,
And she exhorted, in prophetic glow,
The world to wake, and liberty to know.
Of nations grandly moving to the van,
She joined America to honor man.
But O, she trampled on the Crucified,
And all allegiance to Heaven denied.
The arm Divine, which lovingly upheld,
With insult and derision was repelled.
The bond was cut that bound her to the Throne,
And she essayed the steep ascent alone.
Her fall was certain, for she could not wield
The sceptre of Jehovah. Down she reeled,
And, torn by legions from the pit set free,
She fell, and floundered in a bloody sea.
Then she was bound again, and then her chains
Were slightly loosed, and lightened were her pains.

She crept along the bound of life and death,
And seemed at length to catch a freer breath.
Just then a monster came before her face;
He bowed, and leered, with hideous grimace,
Then took a posture for a tiger-spring,
And with a shriek she fell, a breathless thing.

Howe'er the cumulated wrongs may mount,
No one of them we'll place to her account;
Nor shall the tyrant force us to forget
The France of old,—the France of La Fayette.
That he should task his diabolic art,
To win all Europe to the traitors' part,
And force a pause which should their triumph mean,
Was that which easily could be foreseen—
Who crushed the government he swore to save,
A much-confiding people to enslave,
And butchered in cold blood a helpless throng,
To make the nation feel that he was strong:
His fiendish sympathy of course was thrown
Where equal guilt proved him no more alone.

An Emperor is reigning, in these days,
Who chooses for his feet imperial ways.
No stench of perjury surrounds his throne;
No blood of women at its base is shown.
'Tis founded in the providence of God;
And he beholds, attentive to his nod,
A mighty-empire—Sixty million souls
With mastery unchecked his will controls.

While yet afar he saw the high estate,
And trembled for the mission's awful weight,
His spirit-ear caught whisperings divine,
And he resolved, "This guidance shall be mine,"
And twenty million freedmen now attest
The keeping of the consecration blest;
While clear it stands, to all unclouded eyes,
That far below him common kingship lies,
Since champions of the Republic hear
His cordial words of sympathy and cheer.

God bless thee, Alexander! May thy days
Be robed in peace, and heavenward all thy ways.
Such glory's offered thee, O, favored one,
As mortal ne'er possessed beneath the sun.
I see thee leading up thy countless host
Where Freedom's leavening can be aided most;
Discovering, with joy no words can paint,
That safety grants the loosening of restraint;
Dispensing, to the limit of thy might,
The love of Truth, and fealty to Right,
And waking expectation of the day
When Russia will not need imperial sway.
The mission Providence vouchsafes to thee,
The highest angel might with longing see.

VIII.

Well knowing that we battle for mankind,
We cannot hear with unaffected mind
The plaudits uttered, or the curses hurled
By any people of the Christian world.
And yet we have not needed to be taught
That by ourselves this battle must be fought.
We bear, with no desire of human aid,
The high necessity upon us laid.
Our faith in God permits no doubt to rise
That victory is our allotted prize;
But we're not blind to forces that oppose—
We know that sin and folly are our foes.

The love of Money, as the child of Hell,
Of course will aid while slavery's lords rebel.
When it was known the Government must die,
Or food and clothing for defenders buy,
A greedy multitude sprang to their feet,
With rotten shoddy, and with tainted meat,
And gladly still, for swelling of their gains,
They see prolonged their bleeding country's pains.
The fear of taxes in some little souls,
Each aspiration, and attempt controls:

The frightful prospect of a dollar lost
Evokes a cry for "Peace at any cost."

In civil, and in military life,
Are high officials panting in the strife
For filthy lucre—that their only care.
Unmindful of the sacred trusts they bear,
And hindering the action of the true,
They wake to life, in spirits not a few,
A questioning o'erladen with distress
If God can righteously bestow success.

And Cowardice, all quivering, and pale,
Is gasping out—"We certainly shall fail.
The Southerners are terrible to fight,
And, though we know the Union cause is right,
We'd better give it up than all get killed,
And do it now, before more blood is spilled."
If in your bosom you begin to feel
That soul-emasculating spirit steal,
Consider patiently if it be well
To aid the op'ning of the "Gates of Hell;"
Then look upon your brothers as they stand
Against the trait'rous rage, unwavering, grand,
Resolved on death, or a triumphant end,
And, in the light of contrast, comprehend
That thing so despicable every way,—
A coward in America to-day.

Impatience, too, comes flustering in, to spoil
The slowly ripening fruits of anxious toil.

If every thing is not performed at once,
The President's a villain or a dunce.
Of time, or means, no need is recognized,
And legal hindrances are all despised;
With hosts invincible, an act of will
Is held enough the Southern vales to fill;
And it is thought of all things most absurd,
To say that more is needed than a word
To make it true, and have creation see
That all the bondmen of the land are free.

The men who have a hobby-horse to ride,
And blind themselves to every thing beside,
At all, whom various interests engage,
Direct the violence of chronic rage.
Thus Phillips, turned a Mephistophiles,
With silver bow, and gracefully at ease,
Lets fly, in turn, at all the chiefs of state,
The polished arrows of a smiling hate;
And thousands thus with vehemence contend
Against the workers of their only end.

And now Stolidity, in Wisdom's chair,
With stately tone, and magisterial air,
Repeats the rule, from which he's never swerved—
That all existing things must be conserved.
'Tis granted that the traitors are to blame,
And their attempt should cover them with shame;
But when you recommend the only blow
Which can suffice to work their overthrow,

Consent Sir Oracle can never give—
"Why, bless me! That is not conservative."

I've heard that, on a time, it came to pass,
A wiseacre, of this delightful class,
By earnest efforts of a score of friends,
Who showed the patience that affection lends,
Attained, at last, a tolerable sense
Of the important fact of difference,
And then admitted that it might be true
To some old things no reverence was due;
And, while religiously some were conserved,
For death of some all spirits should be nerved.
But things so wondrous are extremely rare;
And, when our chief Executive shall dare
To bid an old iniquity expire,
He must expect an ululation dire.

Ye mortals, whom absurdities delight,
A rich repast these men afford your sight;
Behold them gaze, with reverential tears,
At slavery's edifice, all gray with years.
While throes of righteous doom upheave the ground,
To brace the cracking walls they staddle round;
In very deed they're marvellously sage—
Par excellence, the donkeys of the age!

O, yes! the venerable sin conserve;
Stand firmly to your props; strain every nerve.
Let not the land be stripped of Slavery's charms:
Let babes be torn from shrieking mothers' arms;
Let lacerated maids bow down to lust;
Be Bible teachers into dungeons thrust;
Let strong-limbed men, begirt with bowie-knives,

By stealing from the weak sustain their lives.
Let all those millions of the sons of God
Still crouch, and toil, and bleed beneath the rod;
That misery conserve, at any price,
And, O! conserve that ignorance and vice.
Let not the aged parent of our woe
Be murdered by her self-inflicted blow.
Build up, with votes, a high defensive wall;
Let not the organized damnation fall!

   Another force opposing us we find,
With strength of sin and silliness combined.
'Tis party spirit. Once it did befall,
That with a reason, or with none at all,
A vote affirmed that, in the voter's sight,
A certain party then upheld the Right;
And ever since, a lying pride has taught,
That with confession of mistake 'twere fraught
A doubt to cherish of that party's aims,
Or tolerate a hostile party's claims.
The understanding, on this wise befooled,
With patient assiduity is schooled,
In every act of statesmen once opposed,
To see the blackest infamy disclosed.
While thus the understanding lies in wait,
The heart contributes an infernal hate,
Which conquers interest, and self-respect,
And makes all faculties their force direct
Against the measures of the men who strive
To keep endangered Liberty alive.

   Thus demagogues are furnished with a field
Abundant harvests promising to yield.

Perverting noble energies of mind,
For service of good-will to men designed,
With scorning hearts, but most obsequious face,
They fawn upon the ignorant and base;
Vociferating everywhere the lies
Which quickest make the ruling passion rise;
Except where kindred spirits are addressed,
And naked bribery is found the best.
Their preference is always for the wrong,
Which makes the millions weak, the hundreds strong;
But charms so dear has office in their sight,
That for its sake they can support the Right.

O, "fools, and blind!" Can ye no better see
What practices with interest agree?
Your only aim is benefit of self,
But you prefer authority and pelf;
With conscious meanness gnawing at your heart,
When you might have the high-souled patriot's part,—
Might feel the lifting of a Christ-like love—
Might know yourselves all sordidness above,
And working for the welfare of your race,
With approbation of a God of grace.
O, see yourselves! and hide your heads for shame;
Confess that "Blockhead" is your fittest name.

IX.

'Tis time that all Americans should learn,
Of foolishness the features to discern;

And know, where rottenness of heart they find,
Its presence proves a worthlessness of mind.
However single faculties may glare—
Whate'er attractions single traits may bear—
The intellect is feeble that will choose,
For any price, integrity to lose.
Though tall it towers, 'tis built upon the sand,
And, when the flood assails, it cannot stand.

Behold the mind by Wisdom's presence blest!
How searchingly its steady gazes rest
On all that offers, and solicits choice!
Unmoved by melting look, or wooing voice,
Serenely it applies the test of Right,
And ever catches, with far-reaching sight,
And bids depart with resolution strong,
The wretchedness disguised by smiling Wrong.
That man discloses the colossal mind,
Whom no assaults of selfishness can blind:
A cloud of base ideals he sweeps away,
And, radiant with light of "Perfect day,"
He grasps the high conception of a soul,
With every power at Honesty's control.

To him, when hangs in doubt a nation's fate,
Let Providence assign the helm of state.
The questions which disturb the little mind,
A swift, irrevocable answer find.
Whate'er concerns his interest alone

Is from the field of vision sternly thrown;
He wastes no thought, be pressure e'er so strong,
On what 'tis plain Jehovah views as wrong;
No urgency of need in question draws
The claims of Constitution or of laws;
The oath he took, 'tis settled once for all,
Will not be broken though the heavens fall.
Of all the questions that distraction yield,
And mists illusory, thus cleared the field,
The forces of his intellect are bent,
With singleness of longing, and intent,
To know what righteous acts will most redound
His country's weal immovably to ground.

Rejection falls upon the partly true;
For duty claims a comprehensive view.
No cure is chosen for a present need,
A swarm of troubles afterwards to breed.
Nor hast'ning zeal, nor strong desire of rest
Makes choice prevent revealing of the Best.
No pride, nor prejudice distorts the sight,
But all is seen in dry, veracious light.
As footing indestructible is laid,
The irretraceable advance is made.
The steps are measured well till he can feel
The nation clasping, as with hands of steel,
An everlasting rock on which to stand,
And firmly holding the almighty hand.
Like Samson then he bows with all his might,
And, when his forehead meets descending light,

Among the nations, as they sink and rise,
His own is lifted nearest to the skies.

To these proportions may expand the soul,
Which gives to Honesty its due control.
In light of such a majesty of mind,
What despicable pigmies do we find
All great ones of the Macedonian style,
And all the gods of vision-warped Carlyle!

Indeed America is dear to God.
The strokes He deals are with a Father's rod.
He loves America; already twice
This greatness has become her safety's price,
And He has paid it—O, it must be true
That while He tries, He keeps her good in view,
And what by Honest Washington He gave,
By Honest Lincoln He designs to save.

X.

As round the Leader, at the nation's birth,
Were gathered many of his like in worth,
So he, who now must act the highest part,
On every side finds unison of heart.
While accident, and overhasty zeal
Each day, for strife, a new pretext reveal,

A proud, republic-hating world to face,
And make it plain that measureless disgrace
Would mark an armed espousal of their cause,
Who trample under foot all sacred laws,
The mind of Seward with its gaze profound
Each question piercing to its deepest ground,
And, causes held in philosophic view,
Forethinking certainly what must ensue,
Obeys a heart which high affections fill,
And executes the mandates of a will
Which forty years have proved no power can draw
From rev'rent keeping of the "Higher Law."

And Chase brings up his massive intellect,
To hold the nation's credit still erect,
That patriots, who march against the foe,
The comfort of beloved ones may know;
And Stanton bears his war-advancing part
With all the fervor of an earnest heart,
And fruitful vigor of a mind that knows
The conqu'ring power of unremitting blows;
While Governors their lofty stations fill
With watchful zeal, and loyalty of will,
And hundreds follow the Republic's call
At bureau, or in legislative hall,
O, would that each who holds a public trust,
Were loyal, brave, intelligent, and just;
Americans! Let these be your demands,
Of all who ask for office at your hands:
Bid them, before in their behalf you move,

Their Honesty beyond all question prove;
And claim the showing of a strength of mind,
Which will permit no party-chains to bind;
No scheme to charm because 'tis old, or new;
No love nor hate to overcloud the true.
Who plainly thus are strong in rectitude,
And with a quenchless country-love endued;
To them commit the weighty cares of state,
While brilliant scoundrels you abominate.

The justice of the Government secured,
Of God's protection is the land assured.
How fully proved is this! With what amaze
Each thoughtful mind regards His wondrous ways
To us-ward! Slavery's hell-begotten frame,
The patriot's horror, and the nation's shame,
Was fenced with laws and constitutions round,
And rulers hating her by oaths were bound,
Howe'er their sympathetic hearts might bleed,
To let her foul atrocities proceed;
But He, whose favors on the just descend,
And who from the beginning sees the end,
Decreed the shielding barrier's overthrow,
Exposed the monster to a fatal blow,
And caused the arm, by sacred oath withheld,
By might of that same oath to be impelled.
Then fell the blows upon the hideous head;
And Slavery's dying; she is almost dead.
Let Honesty work on, and we shall see
America's inhabitants all free;

Then love to her may copiously gush,
Be choked by no remorse, and wake no blush.

   Is there a soul, which feels no thrilling strange
At every thought of this stupendous change?
Four millions of immortal ones emerge
From Slavery's darkness. Standing on the verge
Of Freedom's luminous domain, their eyes
Are dazzled by the splendor of her skies.
The narrow paths they cannot yet discern ;
They see not clearly where to step, or turn.
They must be guided. Sweet-voiced, patient love
Shall train their wavering eyes to look above ;
And beams of soft, celestial, healing light
Shall nourish, and invigorate their sight ;
And they shall see that paths, which may be trod,
Converge, and centre at the Throne of God.

   My sable brothers, new-born freemen, hail!
'Tis yours to prove how truthlessly they rail,
Who fix, as far below the white man's race,
In being's scale your God-appointed place.
The work is well begun—That men you are,
Port Hudson, Wagner, Milliken declare,
The Afric blood, in rivulets that ran,
For all your brows is made the seal of man.
Arise, and grasp the virtues of the free ;
Ascend the spirit-feeding heights you see ;
For you, as for us all, an open field
The harvest earned impartially shall yield.

For preservation of that field we fight—
That every child of Adam has a right,
Below the right of none, to sow and reap,
And, unrestricted, virtue's fruits to heap,
The winners of our independence taught.
For that high principle our fathers fought;
For that our brothers have poured out their blood;
For that we offer still the crimson flood.
The orphan's wail, the parent's moan resound;
The weeds of widowhood rise thick around;
We see the countless tokens of distress;
But still we falter not; still on we press;
For, God be witness, we will not concede,
That birth to mastery is mankind's need.

XI.

Say'st thou, poor seeker of a lordling's smile,
" The populace are ignorant and vile,
And, left with no aristocratic sway,
To savageness would quickly fall away?"
'Tis possible the land which gave you birth,
Is yet too poor in Freedom-fostered worth,
By incubus of rank too long oppressed,
In sudden levelling to find her Best.
If so, we counsel you to wait awhile,
Till your compatriots become less vile;
But, as for us, we fortunately know,

Americans are not depressed so low,
That they must feel the whip, and spur, and rein,
Or headlong rush to seize on greater pain.
Calamities are on us now, 'tis true.
From hatred of equality they grew;
And soon shall perish that exotic bane,
And blood of equal freedom, through each vein,
America shall throw from her strong heart,—
A free Republic in her every part,
Presenting, far and near, the forms of good,
Which now arise where she is not withstood.

But you reply : "Though it be fully shown,
A Government may stand without a throne,
Or difference of rank, and exercise
An undisputed sway both mild and wise,
I still maintain a monarchy's the best;
By that alone can glory be possessed."
We freely grant in some things you excel :
Upholstering you do extremely well;
And coronets you have, and jewels rare,
And coats-of-arms devised with patient care.
In ceremonies you are deeply versed;
You know what station in the circle's first,
And when to back, advance, or smile, or bow,
And when to speak, and when to go, and how.
I mean, to some of you these things are known,
While most a slightly different culture own :
The men, whose lives present no princely charms,
Can crouch, and hold their hats beneath their arms.

Or, is the glory, so extremely prized,
That which is gained by forces centralized,
Then poured upon another people's head,
That national dominion may be spread?
We covet no such glory; for we hold
The man, who takes his neighbor's life for gold,
Is but an infant in the course of guilt,
Compared with him, at whose command is spilt
The blood of thousands for no higher end,
Than empire of a nation to extend.

Is glory in commercial greatness sought?
With glory is a people's richness fraught?
In all its fulness we declare it won
By deeds which free Americans have done;
And, if it vitally concern that end,
To ward attacks, and threatened rights defend,
Undoubtingly for this the men we trust,
To each of whom an enterprise unjust,
Against his country's Government, is known,
As menacing the basis of his throne.

But these are trifling things. The arm Divine
Upholds the world with loftier design:
Around the blazing orb this planet rolls,
To gather genial warmth for growing souls.
All earthly ends beside were wisely missed
That noble men and women might exist;
Nor ought a government, in any land,
Ignoring this design, one day to stand.

And here we base our Constitution's claim;
'Tis this that makes us love Republic's name.
With joy, and thankfulness, we recognize
The high deservings of the good and wise,
Whose massive intellects, and moral worth,
Have glorified the monarchies of earth.
Creative power is able to impart
A rare nobility of mind and heart,
Whose God-ward impulse all the chains will burst
Which can be wrought, though sin perform its worst.
But this prerogative is seldom used;
And minds by governmental power abused,
As consequence, will in the main reveal
Deformities no human art can heal.
Now tell me, when all institutions say,
"The many are created to obey,
And hopelessly to labor, that the few
In idleness may count all joys their due;
And birth should designate each person's class,
And build a barrier which none may pass,"
Is there not danger, both to low and high,
In plastic operation of that lie?

Behold his lordship through the gaping throng,
As through a herd of cattle, stalk along:
Conceit of ranking with a higher race
Controls each step, and reigns upon his face.
Can right affection in the hearts abide,
Where forms of government beget such pride?
Whatever in that attitude can place

A man before the millions of his race,
Does it not tend, with most appalling weight,
To crush from human souls each noble trait?

And what's the influence the lowest feel?
Is it conducive to the spirit's weal
To think one's self, by providential plan,
Assigned a rank below the real man?—
In duty bound to quench celestial fire
And banish every thought of going higher?
Or, if the harrowing suspicion lurk
That all this classing is a human work,
Are not the stimulants of envy strong?
Does bitterness not spring from sense of wrong?

But argument is needless. We all know
From cherished falsehood only ill can flow.
To keep that spirit-blighting force away,
We fight, we suffer, we devoutly pray.
No power shall turn us from that lofty aim;
We will, through all our governmental frame,
To this eternal truth its right accord:
THERE'S NO RESPECT OF PERSONS WITH THE LORD.

XII.

Poor Harry Brougham, wrecked by rushing years,
Or spoiled by numbering with British peers,
Asserts 'tis due to vanity alone
That this Republic is not overthrown.
If it be vanity,'while Slavery stands,
With lifted blade, to cleave the Union's bands,
And bids us own our fathers greatly erred
When equal freedom in their bosoms stirred,
And grant their project shamefully has failed,
And Monarchy's pretensions have prevailed,
And yield consent, upon the soil they gave,
And where they bade the starry banner wave,
To rule of potentates, who boldly say,
Upon the weak the strong may rightly prey,—
If it be vanity, at such a time, to rise,
And vow before the Sovereign of the skies,
We'll give our blood, and suffer all the woe
A human being righteously may know,
Ere Slavery that supremacy shall gain,
Then we're convicted as extremely vain.

O, righteous Heaven! Dwells in lying laws
Depraving force which can such blindness cause?

Are men as impotent as they pretend
To form conception of our struggle's end?
Can they be sightless to the glory-blaze
Around the picture that enchains our gaze?
Beyond the billows of this raging flood,
Beyond the battle-smoke, and pouring blood,
A continent reflects the mellow light
Which Peace bestows to glad the spirit-sight.
A people there, for number as the sand,
In dignity of conscious manhood stand.
To boons deserved each knows his rightful claim,
And each to every one accords the same.
As years roll on, 'tis better understood,
That worth of soul is the substantial good.
The artisan, and tiller of the soil,
Combine profound research with daily toil;
And every calling weightily is fraught
With potent stimulants to patient thought.
Throughout the land the minds are multiplied
Which love the wisdom of the Crucified,
And widen their capacities to take
The richness of the words which Jesus spake.
And thus benignly on the Gospel goes:
Though Satan still, and selfish hearts oppose,
The fruits of truth and righteousness increase,
And millions rise from earthly paths of peace,
Well disciplined, along celestial ways,
By deeds of love to swell the Father's praise.

If, while our hearts declare these things must be,
Though joy from all this generation flee,

The habitants of Earth mistake our aim,
And count our glory an eternal shame,
We know, the witnesses who sit above
Are viewing us with approbative love.
I see them floating on a rosy cloud,
To greet a rising band, their faces bowed;
The joyous movements of the comers tell
That where their upward flight began 'tis well.
Now bubbles forth, from smiling lips, a tale,
Which proves America's true sons prevail;
And, when the pleasing narrative is done,
All gazes centre on the face of one;
With love-enkindled eyes, and glowing cheeks,
Serene, the Father of his country speaks:

"The blessedness ineffable is ours,
To see the baffling of Satanic powers.
The prayers of patriots have reached the Throne.
Once more the saving potency is shown
Of Christian truth, whose inspiration strong
Empowered so many of this ransomed throng,
To dare, endure, and all to sacrifice,
That Liberty's impartial sun might rise,
And which so many of these lately slain,
In self-surrendering, have made their gain.
We may believe America accords
So much of reverence to the Lord of lords,
That he will, hence, commission her to teach
The deathless rights of one are rights of each.
Our Father grants the hope that we shall see
Her multiplying millions truly free;

That bonds of ignorance will fall away,
And cruel chains of wickedness decay;
His kingdom come, His righteous will be done,
And glorified the Father and the Son.
O, God is good! unspeakable His grace
To Earth's infatuate, rebellious race!"

Advancing waves of glory meet my sight,
The scene is flooded with a golden light;
Supernal melody the welkin fills.
The cloud of blest ones quiver with its thrills.
They rise; they sink; they're borne upon the tide;
On billows of entrancing sound they ride;
The blended voices of the countless throng
Ecstatically pour in blissful song.

The vision melts away! The anthem dies.
On earth we stand; not yet surmount the skies.
But this I know: there is a spirit-life
Beyond the scenes of sin-begotten strife;
I know that fleshly clogs will lose their force,
And God-like stirrings have unhindered course;
I know, if schooling for that life be gained,
In work for God the spirit must be trained;
I know, because He loves the human race,
And views iniquity with frowning face,
And smiles on them that struggle for the Right,
My country's cause is precious in His sight.

www.ingramcontent.com/pod-product-compliance
Lightning Source LLC
Chambersburg PA
CBHW021939160426
43195CB00011B/1145